AN INTERACTIVE GUIDE TO . . .

Inviting God's Presence

Larry Keefauver, D.Min.

WARNER FAITH

WARNER BOOKS

An AOL Time Warner Company

Unless otherwise noted, Scriptures are taken from the NEW KING JAMES VERSION. Copyright © 1979, 1980, 1982, Thomas Nelson, Inc., Publishers.

Scriptures noted NIV are taken from the HOLY BIBLE: NEW INTERNATIONAL VERSION®. Copyright © 1973, 1978, 1984 by International Bible Society. Used by permission of Zondervan Publishing House. All rights reserved.

Scriptures noted KJV are taken from the King James Version of the Bible.

Scriptures noted TLB are taken from *The Living Bible,* copyright © 1971. Used by permission of Tyndale House Publishers, Inc., Wheaton, Illinois 60189. All rights reserved.

Scriptures noted RSV are taken from the REVISED STANDARD VERSION of the Bible. Copyright © 1949, 1952, 1971, 1973 by the Division of Christian Education of the National Council of the Churches of Christ in the U.S.A. Used by permission.

Scriptures noted NASB are taken from the New American Standard Bible®, Copyright © 1960, 1962, 1963, 1968, 1972, 1975, 1977, 1995 by The Lockman Foundation. Used by permission.

Scriptures noted The Message are taken from *The Message: The New Testament in Contemporary English*. Copyright © 1993 by Eugene H. Peterson.

"Ragman," *Ragman and Other Cries of Faith,* written by Walter Wangerin Jr. Used by permission.

"Breath," written by Marie Barnett. Used by permission.

 An AOL Time Warner Company

Printed in the United States of America

First Warner Books printing: March 2003

10 9 8 7 6 5 4 3 2 1

Library of Congress Cataloging-in-Publication Data
  Keefauver, Larry.
    Inviting God's presence : an interactive guide / Larry Keefauver.
      p. cm.
    "Warner faith".
    ISBN 0-446-67996-8
    1. Spiritual life—Christianity. I. Title.
    BV4501.3.K43 2003
    248.4—dc21   2002033121

Cover design Ann Twomey

Cover photo by Tomomi Saito Photonica

Book design and text composition by Ralph Fowler

CONTENTS

This is the air I breathe,
This is the air I breathe,
Your holy presence,
Living in me.

This is the bread I eat,
This is the bread I eat,
The word of life,
Broken for me.

And I,
I'm desperate for you,

And I,
I hunger for you.

And I,
I'm lost without you.

—Marie Barnett,
    "Breathe"

A RELATIONSHIP WITH GOD IS FAR MORE CRITICAL AND dynamic than the need to know God. Many religious books explore how to know God. This book explores how to experience friendship with God. You can have an intimate, personal relationship with God.

This book offers you the keys to befriending God. It's about:

➤ Relationship, not just knowledge

➤ Trust, not just information

➤ Becoming, not just stagnating

➤ Growing, not just maintaining

➤ Excitement, not just routine

➤ The miraculous, not just the expected

➤ Presence, not just purpose

Life only has purpose when lived in God's presence.

Children, Presence, and Friendship

A S A CHILD, YOU HAD THE UNIQUE ABILITY TO TRUST, believe, accept, and discover reality in innocent and awesome ways. Remember the presence of your invisible, imaginary friend? At times, the hair on the back of your neck stood up when its presence came close. At other moments, your heart raced with joy and anticipation. When no one else could sense your friend's presence, you could. You intuitively knew it was there. Your invisible friend would listen to you for hours on end. Together you would tirelessly play games, inventing imaginary animals, people, and monsters and excitedly enjoying one another's company no matter what you did—or tried to do.

Most important of all, your imaginary friend never hurt you. You could trust it with your most precious secrets, confidently knowing you would never be betrayed. Your friend always:

➤ Told you the truth

➤ Came to your assistance

➤ Helped you

➤ Picked you up when you fell

➤ Made you feel better if you hurt

➤ Gave you a reason to laugh

➤ Hugged you when you were lonely

➤ Wiped away your tears when you were sad

In your imaginary friend's presence you always felt:

➤ Safe and secure

➤ Open and honest

➤ Known and understood

➤ Free and open

➤ Accepted and affirmed

➤ Happy and peaceful

➤ Relaxed and refreshed

The truth is that children often sense the essential presence of a friend far more easily than adults. Perhaps that's why Jesus commented, "I tell you as seriously as I know how that anyone who refuses to come to God as a little child will never be allowed into his Kingdom."[1] Inviting God's presence spiritually starts where all of us naturally start—as children. Children, friendship, presence without guile, and innocence all go together.

Inviting God's presence is a heart quest as desperate as the parched desert sojourner's longing for water or the starved beggar's hungering for a parcel of bread. Inviting God's presence involves what Rudolf Otto called "the holy." For too long holiness has been made unapproachable by religious language and human speculation. We discover as a child that God's holy presence is:

➤ Mysterious—filled with intriguing mystery that draws us into a lifelong search for revelation of ourselves and about God's presence

➤ Tremendous—filled with awe in God's presence for all that God is, including all that the Creator has spoken and willed into being

➤ Fascinating—filled with adoration and passion that continually draws us to the presence of God

Can you remember the mystery you sensed as a child when you gazed into an endless, starlit sky? Can you recall the awe and even trembling you had when you felt a presence enter your room but no one was physically there? Dare you revive that fascination you experienced as a child when you were filled with adoration and wonder in discovering that you could both give and receive love?

Presence can become real when trust knows no limits. With trusting innocence my three-year-old grandson, with eyes shut tight, jumps recklessly into my arms from the side of the pool. No coaxing is necessary. All he needs is to feel my presence close at hand. He never questions my strength to catch him. He never fears the possibility of landing abandoned in the water not knowing how to swim. He never feels any hesitation based on my motives or intentions. My presence is enough to provoke his risk.

So my grandson closes his eyes and leaps into the darkness, laughing while he risks everything in innocent trust believing that in a moment he will be safe in the arms of a loving friend—present just for him. That is a child's reality.

But then it happens. Innocence becomes cluttered with the straw of broken trust, hurtful actions, and angry words. Add to the straw the mud of confusion, disappointment, and unfulfilled expectations. The child shapes emotional and mental bricks that are built into defensive walls of supposed protection to hide behind, fearing real-life friends—even parents—who break promises and betray trust. And just when the child needs them most, some parents become absent.

As a child, you believe the invisible and you trust your instincts to reveal to you truth beyond what you see. But growing into adolescence, you allow your experience to become a mortar that cements together all the bricks of your failures and hurts. No longer do you see creation with awe, wonder, and amazement. Abandoned are your memories of the holy. Instead, you permit the skeptical cynicism of others to taint your innocence and erode your ability to trust. Potential relationships grind to a halt, rusted by fear and doubt. The walls you build to protect yourself from relational hurt become the same walls that distance you from God's presence.

You have come to suppose that God must be the one who ignores you and is too busy for you, much like your dad has been. Or that God nags, cajoles, and manipulates you much like your mom. At best God is absent from your life—not with you when you need him, not caring when you hurt, not present when you move to a new stage of your life.

Perhaps you suppose this God slaps you for every mistake or failure. Or this God rewards you when you're good and beats you when you're bad. Maybe this God has abandoned you much like the mother or father you never knew, becoming for you the Freudian projection of your parents who, though well- or mal-intentioned, simply didn't measure up to your expectations or meet your needs for affirmation or acceptance.

Instead of welcoming God's presence, you cringe at the thought God might draw near to you. Instead of running to him, you have become accustomed to running from him. Mystery no longer intrigues you. Awe mutates from wonder into fear. And fascination with God's presence ceases. Innocence is now replaced by guilt, shame, or doubt. Childhood has been lost in a stormy adolescent sea of unending emotional squalls that now scuttle every relationship with tumultuous highs and lows that threaten to destroy even the most cherished friendships.

Finding most human relationships incapable of sustaining friendship, you have long since abandoned any hope of befriending the invisible or finding God's presence. Lacking trust in those whom you see, how can you believe in what you cannot see? Finding humans to be complex, mysterious organisms of unknowing, how can you find or know One who is Spirit? Recognizing that even the best of earthly friends at some point lies, betrays, and hurts, how can you believe a heavenly being could possibly bridge the abyss between time and eternity to offer you a lasting relationship that does what all others have failed to do?

Have you experienced any of the following walls between you and the presence of God?

> Silence—unanswered prayer

> Mistrust—broken promises and betrayal

> Loneliness—no one with you

> Selfishness—living for yourself

> Confusion—garbled communication

> Anger—unending rage and lethal hostility

> Monotony—life without wonder, signs, or miracles

> Disappointment—unfulfilled expectations

> Despair—hopeless searching

> Unknowing—unfathomable mystery filled with unanswered questions

> Existence—surviving and maintaining but never truly living

> Pain—fearing rejection and punishment

> Greed—always taking while never giving

> Guilt—painful memories of past shame and failure

> Unworthiness—unable to realize your potential

> Legalism—discovering the rules are impossible to obey

Such walls between you and God make inviting God's presence an impossibility.

However, you can find and be found by the presence of God. God's presence is more than *knowing* God; *it's abiding* in him. Truth be known, you were created to be the habitation of the presence of God.

You can know someone and not want to be with that person. You can know the habits and thought of others, their opinions and prejudices, their hopes and dreams, their failures and weaknesses, all without being a friend to them. Knowing another never offers enough material to build a bridge of intimate presence. In fact, the more you know some people, the less you want to befriend them.

Others may promise you how to know God. But what you deeply and intimately need is to personally find the presence of God and abide there.

Know this: God's presence does not dwell in building, temples, synagogues, mosques, or churches. St. Paul reflects: "God, who made the world and everything in it, since He is Lord of heaven and earth, does not dwell in temples made with hands."[2] Yes, you may encounter the presence of God in a location but only because God is everywhere. As an ancient songwriter penned, "Where can I flee from Your presence? If I ascend into heaven, You are there; If I make my bed in hell, behold, You are there."[3]

This book is about relationship, not just knowledge; trust, not just information; becoming, not just stagnating; growing, not just maintaining; excitement, not just routine; the miraculous, not just the expected; presence, not just purpose. Life lacks enduring and eternal purpose without the presence of God. This book offers you the keys to befriending God, the keys to tearing down the walls. Inviting and finding God's presence will uncover the dazzling treasures of:

➤ Communication

➤ Trust

➤ Companionship

➤ Loyalty

➤ Miracles

➤ Expectation

➤ Hope

➤ Revelation

➤ Healing

➤ Cleansing

➤ Acceptance

➤ Strength

As a child again, you can experience the presence of an invisible friend who is always there for you. The passionate, personal pursuit of God's presence will result in a relationship in which there is:

➤ Someone there for you

➤ Someone near to you

➤ Someone listening to you

➤ Someone understanding you

➤ Someone unconditionally loving you

➤ Someone walking with you

➤ Someone forgiving you

Experiencing God's presence starts where you began, without dragging the baggage of where you've been. God's presence allows you to become a unique child instead of forcing you to act like all other adults.

Pursuing God's presence transports you to the other side of loneliness, the other shore of despair. God's presence empowers you to be who you are created to be instead of what others want you to be.

Inviting God's presence brings you to the end of talking to yourself and to the start of a constant companion to talk with. God's presence initiates a relationship that cannot end and will never be broken. Say good-bye to broken friendships, shattered relationships, absent idols that only look at you with empty stares, and one-sided partnerships in which you do all the giving and they do all the taking.

As you journey through this interactive guide, take a few moments each day to write down your responses. After five days, spend your sixth day as a day of reflection, and then on the seventh day rest, refreshed. Don't rush. Inviting God's presence takes time.

Passionately pursue God's presence and find God on the other side of your walls.

Tearing Down the Walls of Silence and Mistrust

*I am so weak that I can
hardly write,
I cannot read my Bible,
I cannot even pray.
I can only lie in God's arms
like a little child,
and trust.*

—James Hudson
Taylor

Introduction

THE PYRAMID-SHAPED ZIGGURAT ROSE SOME SEVENTY FEET OUT of the desert floor before him. Its mud-brick core and fired-brick shell rose defiantly up toward the heavens. At its summit was a shrine to Nannar, the moon god. And all of Ur, capital of Mesopotamia, came to this place seeking an encounter with the numinous.

With piercing eyes, the aging patriarch pondered his religious traditions. The priests had spoken and sung ancient tales of many gods, endless cosmic wars, and men controlled by the deities like puppets on strings—dancing, jumping, falling, and loving at the whims of capricious spirits and mindless forces, all enslaving humanity in a tiresome cycle of endless sacrifices and rituals.

Wearied by religion, all of Abram's soul cried out for relationship. As he gazed wishfully into the expanse of stars on this night of the new moon, his gaunt, weathered face formed a puzzled bust with deep lines sculpted by the invisible finger of loneliness. Rituals gave no answers to the whys of existence. Religion offered no hope for life's despair. And the gods were silent in spite of the priest's desperate incantations and incense offerings.

But Abram sensed a presence permeating the universe into which he gazed. With awe, he pondered the mystery of existence and felt himself fascinated and drawn to an invisible One whose presence was real and approachable.

As you journey with Abram, the friend of God, take a few moments each day to write down your responses. After five days, spend your sixth day as a day of reflection, and then on the seventh day rest, reflect, and refresh. Let me remind you again. Don't rush. Inviting God's presence takes time.

Available to Pursue God's Presence

A S ABRAM STOOD BEFORE PHYSICAL ZIGGURATS, YOU have stood before the cultural ziggurats of money, fame, power, and sex, wondering what you had to sacrifice next to find a friend. Yes, some friends came to your aid when you needed them, but compared to what you had invested, their assistance fell far short of the expected return. They took more than they gave. As your money dwindled, your fame tarnished, your power faded, and your youthful lusts waned, the number of reliable friends diminished proportionately. When the currency of your availability became devalued by time or circumstance, their use for you quickly diminished. Friends seemed to recede like the tide. When you needed their presence the most, they seemed forever absent, busy with their own pursuits.

Even when a high tide of relationship carried you to higher expectations and greater hope, the best of friends failed to have lasting power through the tough crises of life. Many friendships started strong, like a sprinter rushing headlong toward the finish line. However, the friend you needed would have had to be a marathoner. Your sprinter friends started strong but finished weak.

Is there a friend who will run the whole race with you and finish strong? Consider for a moment the qualities you imagine a true friend possessing.

The five most important qualities I look for in a true friend are

1. _____

2. _____

3. _____

4. _____

5. _____

Often you put your ear to the train track, hoping to hear the sound of an approaching engine pulling a trainload of friends who will be there when you need them. Straining to hear the slightest sound or the faintest refrain, you silenced your pounding heart so a sound from anyone out there might be captured and relished as a friendly voice in the damning silence. Was there someone present beyond the silence?

I have noticed that my extroverted grandson has difficulty enduring silence for any length of time. When the TV is turned off and the radio or CD player is mute, he begins his private, personal quest for response. Should no one in the room be speaking to him, he begins to talk to himself. At first, he whispers questions hoping someone or something might respond. Then he sings. It's as if he's trying to prime the well of silence with his own words, vainly hoping to evoke a response. When no one answers, my grandson finally blasts the stillness with the reverberating question so many have asked through the ages, "Is *anyone listening* to me?"

Gazing into the same sky centuries later that Abram peered into, you join the patriarch, asking the question so many have pondered over the centuries: Is anyone there? Is someone there for me? Is anyone listening?

Silencing the voices around and within me, I hear

_____

_____

_____

KEYS TO INVITING GOD'S PRESENCE

🗝 Listen to inspirational music and focus your attention on hearing God.

🗝 Choose a favorite Scripture passage such as, "Be still and know that I am God."[1] Find a comforting, serene place to sit, kneel, or lie down. Remove all outside distractions. (For example, turn off the TV, phone, radio, stereo, or computer.) Becoming perfectly still, tense each set of your muscles in turn, relaxing and breathing deeply after each set. Each time you slowly inhale, think, "Be still." As you slowly exhale, think, "And know that I am God." Silence all distracting voices within you that allow your thoughts to wander. Take five or more minutes to do this. As you meditate, listen only to the thoughts or images that the passage inspires.

○╼ Read from a devotional or inspirational book that uplifts you and fixes your attention on God. Some possible resources include *My Utmost for His Highest* by Oswald Chambers, *Disciplines for The Inner Life* by Bob and Michael V. Benson, and *Lord Hear Our Prayer* by Thomas McNally and William G. Storey. After reading for about five minutes, stop and reflect on what you have read. In a journal, jot down your thoughts about God. Especially listen to those thoughts that are fresh and encouraging.

———⊗⊗⊗———

Pursuing God's presence requires availability.

The Wall of Silence

Wᴀᴛ ɪꜰ ᴛʜᴇʀᴇ ᴡᴀꜱ ꜱᴏᴍᴇᴏɴᴇ ᴏᴜᴛ ᴛʜᴇʀᴇ ʙᴇʏᴏɴᴅ our world and he was not silent? Yet when he spoke no one listened. Imagine decades passing and God's presence calling out for just one child, one man, one woman to reply. Like a street preacher shouting sermons on a sidewalk to countless passersby who refused to make eye contact or slow their gait, God perched on the edge of eternity's precipice and called out, "Hey, you, need a friend?"

Nomads and caravans of traders passed through the desert day after day, peddling their goods across the Fertile Crescent from the Indian subcontinent to Egypt. None heard the voice. City dwellers in Ur and Haran shaped their pots, carved their wood, and traded their crafts. None heard the voice.

Busy with the chores that filled their lives, the ancients were more like us than we might imagine. Stress hampered and hindered them as it does us. Even if God had walked down the narrow streets and shopped in the open air market, few would have stopped to notice him as anything other than a customer. They were selling; he was buying. Inviting God simply wasn't part of the equation.

How many had God approached before that fateful starlit night when Abram stood alone before the cosmos wondering if someone was there for him? How many had failed to hear the quiet whisper of one who could only be heard if all other voices were silenced?

That is the key: Friendship requires *listening*—suppressing the roar of the crowd or the din of inner turmoil. Being in God's presence demands verbal intercourse, giving and taking, not always talking. But you have had only enough time for stringed-together, staccato monologues that pose as counterfeit dialogues:

"I want a Number One."

"Combo? Drink with fries?"

"Okay."

"Supersized?"

"Sure."

"Something to drink with that?"

"Diet Coke."

"That's four ninety-five. Pull up to the first window to pay."

Instead of talking *with* others, you talk *at* others, like speaking into a box at the drive-through window. You talk to get something from them, all the while completely uninterested in their needs or concerns.

Consequently, you never get to know other people. Your conversations are with strangers—you want something from them or they need something from you. Like parallel railway tracks, no connection is possible; there is nothing more than an occasional solitary tie making a momentary connection for exchange. Nothing personal transpires. Proximity, not presence, has occurred; you only experience emptiness.

You have learned an eternal truth in the passionate, personal pursuit of God: Proximity alone cannot equate with presence.

When someone is truly present and there for me, that person

_____

_____

_____

Pursuing God's presence must be more than having two parallel monologues. Pursuing his presence is not simply trying to get something from him while paying the cheapest possible price in obedience. You can't think of interaction as simply, "How much penance must I do to correct this wrong? How many prayers must I deposit like coins in a slot machine before the winning answer comes out?"

The truth of the matter is this: Many hunger desperately for God's presence, but only a few will passionately pursue him. In spite of all the pious-sounding words or religious language, few take the time or have the inclination to listen. Recognizing this, Jesus remarked, "But the Gateway to Life is small, and the road is narrow, and only a few ever find it."[2]

You have begun the journey of finding God's presence. And therefore you have begun to realize that in our culture, like Abram's, many are so busy *doing* that no time is left for *becoming*. *Religion*—as opposed to *relationship*—is nothing more than doing. If you are doing something for God, you expect God to be doing something for you. But what's exchanged through doing is nothing more than "stuff." Pursuit has become the end, not the means; you are doing in order to get. Your expectations are:

➤ I give money; God gives money back.

➤ I do good; God blesses me.

➤ I obey his commands; God rewards me after this life.

All this smacks of religiosity, teetering dangerously close to the edge of hypocrisy's cliff.

Religions abound for the doers. But only relaters find God's presence. If religion is about doing, relationship is about being and becoming. Spiritual intimacy requires friendship. In Abram's day as today, God looked for a friend, not an employee, partner, investor, or customer. God wasn't interested in a franchise or a public offering; he simply wanted a friend to abide in his presence—someone to talk with. With the days and months turning into years, God's presence moved through time with grace. He sought one who would listen—one who might carry on a dialogue instead of retreating to a familiar monologue learned at the altar of an idol.

Idols are comforting and decorative but lacking in social skills. They make great statues but serve as poor substitutes for friends. You can talk at them but never with them. You can offer sacrifices but never get responses. One named Elijah found this truth centuries ago. On a wind-swept mount called Carmel, Elijah challenged the prophets of the idol-god Baal to a duel. Believing idols to be friends, the prophets danced, chanted, and cried out to Baal for an answer, but they received only silence. Then Elijah called out to the living God, and fire rained down from heaven. Someone was there, and he was not silent! Elijah walked away as God's friend; the prophets lost the contest and then their lives.

The moral? Religion's hype never satisfies; religion's addiction always requires more and more from you while giving nothing back except exhaustion and death. Relationship is vital.

Inviting God starts with being instead of doing. You've never referred to yourself as a human *doing*, right? Just the opposite is true. You are a human *being*. When two beings talk and listen to one another, the wall of silence is shattered and seeds of a developing friendship are sown.

What must I cease *doing* to start pursuing God's presence?

_____

_____

_____

KEYS TO INVITING GOD'S PRESENCE

⚷ Consider all the ways you are a good friend. Make a list of those ways. Which one of these ways will you try in pursuing God's presence?

_____

_____

_____

⚷ List the things that others do to you that keep you from wanting to be their friends. Decide not to treat God in these ways.

_____

_____

_____

⚷ In the silence, let go of negative thoughts and feelings toward God. Make an effort to begin thinking and feeling positively about God.

———⧈———

Pursuing God's presence bridges silence
with listening and dialogue.

The Wall of Mistrust

Where must you go to find God? If inviting God's presence is just a matter of going somewhere, then simply going to a game, a bar, a club, a social, an event would be all it takes to enter into a friend's presence. But think for a moment. Is it a crowd that you want? Do you want to have to single a friend out of a group? What if you're in the wrong crowd? You could get shackled with someone who might at first look like a friend but in actuality is an enemy.

Friends require screening and individual scrutiny. Why? Because you can't trust everyone you meet—even in the right crowd. Haven't child-abusing priests inhabited some churches? Haven't sexual predators stalked their prey in singles' groups? Whom can you trust to be your friend? With whom can you be alone and feel safe and secure?

My most trusted friends are

_____

_____

_____

Now look over your list and circle the names of those friends who would never let you down or betray you.

How many names did you circle? Fewer than you expected to? Betrayal may have slammed you so often that now you trust no one. Perhaps those who pretended to be your friends stabbed you in the back. And now you've erected a wall of mistrust so no one can "do you in" again. But will the wall of mistrust really protect you? Or will it simply cut you off from the One who would be your true friend?

Try this exercise: Ask someone to stand about an arm's length behind you. Announce to your assistant that on the count of three you will fall with complete trust and abandon into his outstretched arms. Close your eyes. Lock your knees. On the count of three, shift your full weight back, pivoting on your heels and falling recklessly into the arms of the one who is there—unseen, invisible, but surely willing to catch you.

Or is he? And even if he is willing, is he strong enough to keep you from falling?

You may believe a friend would never let you fall. But you have fallen often since childhood. Some of the falls tore at your psyche and shattered your self-confidence and respect. Other falls robbed you of money, time, relationships, and opportunities. Predictably, each fall added another brick to your wall of mistrust. You thought, *If God was there for me, why didn't he keep me from falling?*

But were the falls your fault or God's? More important, even if each fall can be blamed on consequences arising from your own poor judgment or erroneous ways, why didn't God, like a true friend, simply bail you out?

Of course the answer is that true friends don't always bail us out. If they did, we would never learn from our mistakes.

If you feel that God has let you down in the past, then a wall of mistrust and unforgiveness toward him has most likely formed within you. Before you can find God's presence, you must forgive him for not catching you when you thought he should. Of course, the question is not whether or not he should have caught you. The fact is that you had expectations for how God should act in your life . . . and he didn't. Still, even though he did nothing wrong, forgiving him is necessary for your own sake. You expected someone to be there for you, and when that expectation wasn't fulfilled, you began to build your wall. Before you can trust, you must forgive.

My prayer for forgiveness from God for wishing him to be or do what *I* expected is:

_____

_____

_____

If you remember a time when a friend let you down, work on forgiving that friend before trying to forgive God. Lack of forgiveness toward others will be a wall between you and God. If that person is still alive, write a letter, make a call, send an e-mail, or go to them and be reconciled.

Remember a time when a friend forgave you. Quietly begin thanking God for others who have forgiven you. You might pray, "God, I am thankful for _____ who forgave me and made the effort to restore our friendship."

If you feel you have failed to live up to God's expectations of you, be assured that simply by asking for forgiveness, you will receive it. Memorize this promise: "For You, Lord, are good, and ready to forgive, and abundant in mercy to all those who call upon You."[3]

Pursuing God's presence requires us to forgive God
for not living up to our expectations of him.

Moving beyond Mistrust

THE WALL OF MISTRUST FORMS AROUND EXPERIENCES. An experience is simply a set of facts you or I must interpret and give meaning to. Without that sense of perspective to help us understand what has happened, experiences would simply weave through our consciousness without form.

So, if our experiences are the facts, what is the final truth? An investigator at a crime scene accumulates myriad facts. But she must then organize and interpret them to arrive at a premise she believes to be the truth. The same is true of us. Circumstantial evidence in our lives may at times indicate God is not there. Or, if he is, he is temporarily absent, at best, or malevolent, at worse.

Circumstantial evidence never fully paints the picture of his presence. Looking back on our lives, we often see meaning and purpose in past events *after* they have transpired. During those trying and exasperating circumstances we may have felt alone and abandoned by God. But now, in maturity, we know that feelings are real but not always reality.

So with hindsight we come to the realization that God as at work for good in all things. A momentary silence was simply a pause, not an absence. For us, that pause may have seemed unending. But later, we discovered that what seemed so terrible actually worked out for the best and what felt so lonely was actually an imagined and temporary silence birthed by our impatience.

But have you considered the possibility that it is your wall of mistrust that has kept God's presence away? Perhaps you have chosen to believe what you perceived and interpreted instead of listening for his voice and understanding his ways. How then can you move past your preconceived notions and embrace the God who is waiting for you?

If friendship between humans is exacerbating, then how much more frustrating finding God's presence must be! To think that one who is finite can join hands and heart with One who is infinite is quite a stretch. Knowing how easily mistrust arises between humans, how much more the possibility of mistrust between flesh and spirit?

Still, remember that the relationship between what is seen and what is not seen was easily possible as a child. We need to remember that even as adults we have the capacity to see beyond the natural into the supernatural. No fact verifies love, but love is real. No circumstance dictates compassion, but compassion is a truth that transcends the suffering of the innocent. Therefore, even if the facts suggest no one is out there, we need to accept the possibility that God *is* there and we're simply not listening.

The wall of mistrust creates a perception that chooses facts over real truth, stuff over relationship, loneliness over connectedness, and independence over interdependence. Mistrust cries out: "I don't need anyone, especially someone unseen. I can make it by myself. I can perceive facts with my senses. The invisible doesn't exist; the supernatural can never happen; miracles cannot occur. Life is trapped in a box of existence walled in by birth and death and filled with meaningless circumstances."

Finding God cannot happen as long as you choose to live behind this wall of mistrust.

The reasons for which I feel mistrust are (circle any that apply):

- Someone has hurt me.
- Someone has failed to keep a promise.
- Someone has lied to me.
- Someone has violated my trust.
- Someone didn't meet my expectations.
- Someone _____

Deciding to silence your natural perceptions and to question learned worldview dictums will help you tear down the wall of mistrust. On the other side of that wall is One who is not silent, who can be trusted. God's invisible presence, in a quiet and still voice, is saying to you, "I have loved you with an everlasting love."[4]

Before you can enter into God's presence, you must step out and trust his voice. After forgiving him, the next step is moving beyond the fear of what might happen in your relationship. All relationships require us to set aside fear of future hurt. When the pain of loneliness becomes greater than the fear of hurt, we will pursue the presence of God.

When I tear town my wall of mistrust, my greatest fear is

_____

_____

_____

—⊗⊗⊗—

The pursuit of God's presence sets aside fear and
trusts the loving voice of the unseen One.

Tearing Down the Walls

ABRAM SET ASIDE HIS WORLDVIEW THAT THE HIGHEST life he could know was revealed in a tower made of dirt that could never reach the stars. Oh, humanity had tried to build its tower of Babel, hoping to climb from the visible into the invisible. But miscommunication had wrecked human endeavor as everyone spoke rather than listened to the One they so desperately wanted to reach.

Abram's journey into God's presence began with listening and trusting. Penetrating the silence, God spoke, "Leave where you are. Go to a place I will show you."[5] Before presence came listening. Before the promised land of relationship came trusting.

At first, trust comes slowly when Presence presents us with a voice but no face. With only a voice we cannot discern the non-verbal communication of body language, facial expression, gestures, eye contact, touch, and the like. It's hard enough to communicate with trust through e-mail, fax, or even a phone. Only when we see another does trust begin to move from seed to root.

How does one follow an unseen, faceless voice to a new place that one has never been? How does a friendship start between flesh and Spirit?

In order to begin my journey toward trust, I will (circle all that apply):

- Step out from behind my wall of silence.

- Listen to the unseen voice who invites trust.

- Silence every voice that accuses my past, demeans my present, and destroys my future hope.

- Understand that inviting God's presence into my life is based on *being*, not *doing*.

- Know that friendship shatters preconceived notions about what God is like. I will let God's presence reveal his character.

Without the walls of silence and mistrust, you will both hear and trust the voice of the God who is present.

Listen to some of what God's presence is saying to you:

➤ Listen and hear my voice; pay attention and hear what I say.

➤ My sheep listen to my voice; I know them, and they follow me. I give them eternal life, and they shall never perish; no one can snatch them out of my hand.

➤ I will save you; you will not fall by the sword but will escape with your life, because you trust in me.[6]

Tearing down the walls of silence and mistrust means that I will become

_____

_____

_____

KEYS TO INVITING GOD'S PRESENCE

🗝 Write down the last positive, encouraging thing that happened to you during an extended time of silence.

_____

_____

_____

🗝 Remember a time when someone forgave you for hurting him or her in a friendship. Quietly begin thanking God for others who have forgiven you. You might pray: "God, I am thanking you for _____ who forgave me and made the effort to restore our friendship."

If you feel you have failed to live up to God's expectations of you, be assured that simply by asking for forgiveness, you will receive it. Memorize the promise: "For You, Lord, are good, and ready to forgive, And abundant in mercy to all those who call upon You."

*The journey of inviting God's presence
begins with tearing down the walls
of silence and mistrust.*

Tearing Down the Walls of Silence and Mistrust

I stopped listening for the voice of God when

_____

_____

_____

I ceased trying to talk with God when

_____

_____

_____

A wall of silence supposedly protects me from

_____

_____

_____

I decided not to trust God's presence when

_____

_____

_____

The voices *inside* me that must be silenced so I can hear God are

_____

_____

_____

The voices *around* me that must be silenced so I can hear God are

_____

_____

_____

The first step I must take toward trusting the presence of God is

_____

_____

_____

Listening to God requires me to be

_____

_____

_____

Trusting God requires me to be

_____

_____

_____

∽∽∽

In order to passionately pursue God's presence,
I need to return to childlike trust.

Tearing Down the Walls of Loneliness and Selfishness

*Self is the opaque veil
that hides the face of
God from us.*

—A. W. TOZER

Introduction

SEPARATION FROM THE WOMB SOWS THE POTENTIAL SEEDS OF loneliness. No longer are we connected and attached, surrounded and protected by the ones who conceived us. Immediately a search for relationship begins. Survival itself depends on it, for without intimacy no one is there to hold us. Without relationship no one is there to feed us. Without presence no one is there to speak into our lives. Yes, for some, a parenting figure still provides intermittent contact with another. Tragically for others, no parent is there. Perhaps a surrogate feeds and nurtures. But for some, there is not even that. And anyway, the best a parent can do is prolong the inevitable realization that we are separated. The warmth and security of the womb has vanished forever.

As newborns, we are self-centered. The world revolves around our immediate needs. And when we don't get what we want, we cry out, demanding a response. Sensing the presence of a parent or other nurturer draw near, we cry even louder with piercing intensity. At times, our needs are real. We are hungry, wet, hurting, or unstimulated. We need someone there to do for us what we can't do for ourselves.

Later in life, we may continue to think someone else should meet all of our wants. We may even envision God to be a Freudian father figure or the fanciful incarnation of a cosmic Santa Claus who meets our wants whenever we pitch a temper tantrum. In essence, such a god only exists in our fancies and we pretend he is there to satisfy our every whim. Yet we know that such a doting, spiritual slave doesn't exist. We may rage at the silence or bitterly denounce all theism with supposed atheism or indifferent agnosticism. Yet we know deep within ourselves that the presence we seek will never meet our never-ending wish list of wants and needs.

Inviting God's presence is never predicated on our wants or self-centered lusts and desires. Wanting never promotes a transcendent response nor does a demand force a reluctant answer. His presence is always found in his way, on his terms, and by his prerogative.

Out of the silence comes a whisper: *This plan of mine is not what you would work out; neither are my thoughts the same as yours! For just as the heavens are higher than the earth, so are my ways higher than yours, and my thoughts than yours.*[1]

Unsatisfied, we decide to build our walls of loneliness and selfishness. We decide to punish the One who is there for us with separation and self-absorption. However, believing or acting that his presence is not there doesn't make the Presence disappear. And continually focusing on self doesn't remove the Presence from proximity. If a friend sits in a waiting room desiring to see me, my ignoring her doesn't make her presence any less real. If a friend refuses to do for me what I want, my rejection of and isolation from him doesn't alter his pursuit of me.

On the other side of my lonely wall, God's presence waits. On the perimeter of my inward gluttony, his presence camps out, hoping I might move from the place where "I" pretends to be the only reality and to the place where "We" can find relationship.

This week, you will begin to recognize and then dismantle the walls of loneliness and selfishness. While removing these walls cannot ensure relationship, allowing the walls to remain guarantees the absence of knowing and being known, of finding and being found.

Hiding from His Presence

Mistaking ourselves for the Presence, we deny our loneliness and believe that we alone are gods. Creating a wall of self-centeredness or selfishness, we limit our perception to only what we can sense: hear, taste, touch, see, and smell.

But we are not the Presence. God's presence existed before our senses could perceive and deny him. Presence existed before sense. Is not presence also *pre-sense*? Consider your origins.

Before you could sense his touch, God touched and formed you. Reaching into the formless clay, his presence shaped you into his image. Looking into the mirror of eternity, he formed you to be the vessel of his presence.

Before you could touch anything, God created texture so that everything touched might be felt. His presence formed your ability to touch and be touched so that he might touch you. In fact, the first touch humanity experienced was the hand of his presence modeling clay into human form.

Before you could hear, a word was spoken: "Let us make humans in our image."[2] Out of that word came shape, form, destiny, purpose, and life. Without the word, nothing would exist. The word brought being out of nonbeing and created the animate from the inanimate. Prior to hearing, the word gave you the capacity to hear.

Before you could see, God's presence saw that both you and your environment would be good. And he saw that it was good. Before you saw, all of the universe was created so that when you could see, an infinite, starry night would await you. Before light ever moved through your cornea and struck your retina's cones and rods, a rainbow of color painted myriad flowers, creatures, plants and rocks for your sight to behold and enjoy.

Before you could taste, the sweet and the sour, the hot and the cold, the subtle and the sublime of tastes were prepared to fill your palate with any taste you could imagine.

Before you could smell the delicate fragrance of a flower or the pungent odor of a skunk, the smells existed and awaited your discovery.

And all of the tastes, sights, sounds, smells, and textures were created and pronounced good.

So the vessel—you—was formed. Though Spirit cannot be limited to form, Spirit can fill it. Spirit cannot be the vessel, but it can flow into the vessel. You were created to be filled, not empty; inhabited, not empty; indwelt, not vacant; overflowing, not lacking; and flowing, not dry.

But if you, as the vessel, determine to be self-centered and imagine yourself to be alone in the garden of life, then destiny is thwarted, purpose is forfeited, and relationship is cut off. The temptation "You shall be as god"[3] is a lie, not life. Adopted, such a lie cuts off life and builds a wall of loneliness and selfishness.

Imagine a cupboard filled with glasses that are never filled. Imagine endless rows of pots forever empty. Yes, museums filled with artifacts display the pots and vessels of bygone civilizations. But they were not created to sit on a museum shelf. And you were not created to be placed on a shelf and observed, as if a lifeless vase, by those living.

The purpose and shape of your destiny is not to stay empty and alone. There is an implicit relationship between the container and the contained, the cup and the beverage, the vessel and the substance to be held within. You were created to be indwelt by the very Presence that formed you. You were formed for relationship not loneliness and for indwelling not emptiness.

My purpose in being is

_____

_____

_____

Relationships are

_____

_____

_____

I feel empty when

_____

_____

_____

Religion beckons you to empty yourself and thus find yourself. Should you heed that call, you will find you are empty, lost, and alone. Inviting God's presence calls you to a journey of rediscovering your created purpose and destiny. The lie says you are alone. The truth is life. Life is the discovery that he is there, waiting and open to you.

And they heard the sound of the Lord God walking in the garden in the cool of the day, and Adam and his wife hid themselves from the presence of the Lord God among the trees of the garden.[4]

God is always present and never absent. You may be hiding from his presence. Why? It could be guilt, shame, indifference, pain, hurt, or a multitude of other reasons. Yet he is on the other side of your loneliness.

I hide from God's presence because

_____

_____

_____

KEYS TO INVITING GOD'S PRESENCE

- In solitude, examine your feelings. Do you feel alone with God or simply lonely—apart from God's presence? Write down all the feelings you experience when you are alone.

- If most of your feelings about being alone are negative, think back to why you first felt the negativity. Write a letter to God describing your feelings.

- Read the following words written by King David from the ancient Hebrew hymns. Circle phrases that reveal how you are feeling:

My God, my God, why have you forsaken me?

Why are you so far from saving me,

so far from the words of my groaning?

O my God, I cry out by day, but you do not answer,

by night, and am not silent.[5]

Do you find yourself hiding from God? Are there times when you dread the possibility that God might be present to see what you are doing or know what you are feeling? How would you feel if you knew that nothing you thought or did would keep God's presence away from you? Circle words that describe how you feel God may feel toward you.

Angry   Frustrated   Judgmental

Pleased   Accepting   Inviting

If you find yourself lonely and imprisoned by negative feelings that cause you to hide from God, make a decision to let go of the negative feelings. List the negative feelings you will release. Replace the feelings with the desire to come into God's presence.

_____

_____

_____

———⊷∞∞⊶———

I may try to hide from God's presence;
God never ceases seeking my presence.

Rejecting the Lie

Y OUR CHOICE IS BETWEEN LIFE AND LIES. ONE LIE IS that you are all alone in the universe and no one is there for you. Another lie is that you are God and no one is there for you.

Lies are easy to believe when all we have to rely upon is our senses. Our senses tell us that what's real is only what we can touch, smell, taste, see, or hear. But we know better. Reality exists within and beyond our senses.

From our earliest recollections we have known the realities of love, comfort, fear, hate, peace, joy, and a myriad other abstractions that our senses cannot verify. The love of a mother or father, the comfort of a friend, the fear of the unknown, the hate inspired by an enemy, the peace that comes through resolution, and the joy that bubbles out of encountering a friend are all realities we cannot circumscribe.

Yet the enemy of Presence perpetuates charming lies that lead us to doubt and ultimately lead us to loneliness. Examine these four lies:

Existence is life. The first lie perpetuates the poison that existence apart from Presence can be life. At best, existence only mimics life. Existence is only a shadow, while life is the substance. Existence is like a cloud, a vapor, a mist, or a mirage; when we reach out to grasp it all we have in our hands is like a passing breeze that vanishes instantly. Life is lasting; existence is passing. Out of the tree of life springs the fruit that lasts. Out of the tree of the knowledge of good and evil springs existence that, like smoke, dissipates almost as soon as it appears.

The visible is eternal. The enemy would have us believe that what we see lasts forever. We build monuments and memorials, but in time they crumble. We think that trusts, foundations, and endowments will last, but they run their course. Even the memories of our lives fade in the minds of our descendants.

We believe the lie when we are young, for youth believes itself to be immortal. Rarely do we think about death until a friend dies or we age and those around us begin dying. We function with an operative denial of our mortality and rage against any illness or accident that robs the victim of the supposed long life they should have. The truth is that what is seen lacks staying power and what's invisible holds the key to the eternal. "So we fix our eyes not on what is seen, but on what is unseen. For what is seen is temporary, but what is unseen is eternal."[6]

We are as gods. The enemy of God's presence tempts us to believe that we shall be as gods. Again, we cannot be confused at this point. Sigmund Freud's theory that God is simply a projection of our need for a father is not credible. God's presence is not a figment of our imaginations or a projection of our needs. To think that we are gods and there is no Other reduces us to a lonely state. To swallow such a lie reduces us to an existence where all we have to listen to is ourselves. Relationships with others and God become impossible because we are all consumed with self.

Such self-absorption builds a wall of isolation and loneliness not only between God and us but also between us and others. Such a state of being becomes what Martin Buber calls *I-I.* Recognizing the existence of God's presence and entering into relationship with God is an I-Thou relationship. Buber reflects about people consumed with I-I relationships:

> *Some live in a strange world bounded by a path from which countless ways lead inside. If there were road signs, all of them might bear the same inscription: I-I . . . You are not an object for men like this, not a thing to be used or experienced, nor an object of interest or fascination. The point is not at all that you are found interesting or fascinating instead of being seen as a fellow I. The shock is rather that you are not found interesting or fascinating at all: You are not recognized as an object any more than as a subject. You are accepted, if at all, as one to be spoken at and spoken of; but when you are spoken of, the lord of every story will be I.*[7]

Good itself is god. The final lie of the enemy regarding God's presence is that good is God—whenever we pursue a good idea, we will find God's presence. The truth is that the pursuit of good, while initially fruitful, leads us into dead ends and blind alleys. We can never get adequate answers to such questions as:

➤ Who determines what is good?

➤ Is anything purely good without ulterior motive?

➤ What is the standard of good?

➤ Is one person's good another's evil?

In fact, the pursuit of good can so consume us that we never get to the pursuit of God's presence. Pursuing good gives us religion without Presence. The pursuit of good doesn't need God. "Doing good myself" results in a lonely, desperate life of pursuing perfection but never attaining it. Millennia after this lie was first spoken, the truth finally came out: No one is good—except God.[8]

Believing any of these lies builds a wall of loneliness between us and God. Believing these lies drives us to *hide* from God's presence, not *find* his presence. Determine to reject the lies.

The lie that is most tempting for me to believe—and the reason for believing it—is

_____

_____

_____

KEYS TO INVITING GOD'S PRESENCE

🔑 Make a list of all your good ideas for the day. Which are actually from God and which are simply your attempts to be good? Eliminate the good things you do that distract you from God ideas in your life.

🔑 Inviting God's presence requires a willingness within you to reject an I-I attitude toward life. Remember your conversations over the past few days. Are they only focused on yourself? Will you turn your affection away from just yourself and toward God and others?

🔑 Existence is getting by but not really living. On a sheet of paper list everything you did today. Give a percentage to each of the following:

TIME SPENT	PERCENTAGE
Living for myself	_____
To maintain life	_____
With others and for others	_____
Alone with God	_____

Now take fifteen minutes to dream. Visualize the invisible. Instead of focusing on what is, contemplate what can be. Releasing the past and stepping outside the tyranny of the present, allow yourself to dream about God's possibilities for your life. Write down some of those dreams.

_____

_____

_____

Believing that reality only exists in what is seen blinds me to the invisible reality encompassing me.

God's Presence Means Being Face to Face

EVER DREADED LOOKING SOMEONE IN THE FACE? Ever avoided seeing another person?

I recall a time when my relationship with a friend went sour. I couldn't stand the thought of being in that person's presence. Not that they had done anything against me. I had spoken ill of them and the odor of those stinking comments had drifted back to them through others. Once released, words take on a life of their own. And the life of these words wreaked havoc in my relationship with my friend, whom I began to perceive as my enemy.

Instead of restitution, I sought isolation. Fearing I might accidentally run into him, I avoided stores in the area of town in which my former friend lived. What would I say? I would be so embarrassed!

However, the day came that the doorbell rang. Looking out the curtain before opening the door I saw a dreaded sight: my former friend's car. Terror struck deep into my soul. *I must hide! I must pretend I'm not home. I must hide my face.*

My friend refused to abandon me or give up on our relationship. He wanted to restore and continue our friendship. I thought it was less painful to be lonely than to be connected. I was wrong, but it took repentance and forgiveness to discover that the risk of relationship far outweighed the fear of possible pain and hurt.

When the pain of loneliness becomes greater than the fear of face-to-face confrontation, you will pursue a relationship with God.

In the garden of beginnings called Eden, Adam and Eve hid themselves from the presence of God. As a friend, God came to walk with them in the cool of the evening.

Then the man and his wife heard the sound of the Lord God as he was walking in the garden in the cool of the day, and they hid from the Lord God among the trees of the garden. But the Lord God called to the man, "Where are you?"

He answered, "I heard you in the garden, and I was afraid because I was naked; so I hid."[9]

When I hurt or disappoint another person, I (circle all that apply):

- Run

- Hide

- Avoid

- Confess

- Repent

- Excuse

- Rationalize

- Run away from _____

- Run to _____

- Other _____

We would make God's presence abstract and ethereal when in fact it's quite concrete and real. How is that? Let's return to my story about my friend whom I turned into my enemy.

My friend was never my enemy. He remained open, loving, accepting, and friendly toward me. It was I who painted the portrait of my friend as my enemy. After having said unkind things about him, I refused to see him face to face. I imagined him thinking all kinds of ill about me. I envisioned him talking negatively to others about me. And I dreaded a meeting with him for fear I would lose face.

That's exactly what happens when we avoid God's presence. Shame transforms us from openness to closedness. Guilt puts on us the racing shoes labeled, "Get as far away as possible." Embarrassment, or even the thought of it, turn us from lions into weasels. "They hid themselves from the Lord God" literally means "they hid themselves from God's face." When we're wrong, we hate facing the person we've wronged. Face to face, we might have to admit our errors.

To be in the presence of God is simply to be face to face with God. No running. No hiding. No pretending not to be there. The moment of truth has arrived. The time to 'fess up is upon us. We are face to face with God.

The bricks we use to build the walls of loneliness and selfishness between God and us are:

➢ Guilt

➢ Shame

➢ Embarrassment

➢ Fear

When my friend came to the door, I knew he wanted a face-to-face encounter with me. Our relationship could not be restored until I was in his presence, but I did everything in my power to avoid that confrontation.

I pretended he didn't exist. Ever done that with God?

I acted as if I had done nothing wrong. Ever done that with God?

I made excuses for myself to others about what I had done, trying to rationalize my wrongs. Ever done that with God?

I hid out and avoided contact with him. Ever done that with God?

I hide from God because

_____

_____

_____

KEYS TO INVITING GOD'S PRESENCE

➤ Complete these sentences.

I feel guilty when

_____

I feel ashamed when

_____

I feel lonely when

_____

I feel afraid of God when

_____

I feel embarrassed when

_____

🗝 Describe what you say, feel, and do when you sense God may be coming to you.

_____

_____

_____

🗝 If you had been Adam or Eve, what would you have done? Circle one action.

Hide   Run   Excuse myself   Defend myself

Confront God   Ask forgiveness   I don't know

Other _____

———⊗⊗⊗———

*Hiding from God only veils the truth of his
omnipresence from my own eyes.*

Going beyond Self

Abraham Maslow's hierarchy of needs places self-actualization as the ultimate quest of the human journey.[10] Self becomes the pinnacle of life's climb and the depth of life's probing. The modern quest of materialism and self-gratification constantly asks, "What's in it for me?" Every business deal, car deal, house deal, and relational deal seems to ask, "What will I get out of it?" The only relationship selfishness can endure is I-I. An I-Thou relationship cannot be tolerated behind a wall of selfishness.

The wall of selfishness that we build between God and us becomes a mirror blocking our need for a window. It's like being in the carnival's house of mirrors. Everywhere we turn, we see ourselves and nothing else.

After the enemy of God's presence tempted Adam and Eve in the garden, they decided to eat of the forbidden fruit. But why? What came between them and God's presence? Notice what's reported: "The woman was convinced. How lovely and fresh looking it was! And it would make her so wise! So she ate some of the fruit and gave some to her husband, and he ate it too."[11] What was in it for them? Wisdom. The knowledge of good and evil became their pursuit, not the presence of God.

Fixing our eyes on self always limits our vision to the visible and our future to the finite. Without seeing the invisible, we will never do the impossible. As a result, we cannot see God because our eyes are fixed on the fruit, not the One who created and supplied the fruit. We begin to worship the creature instead of the Creator.

My selfishness causes me to

_____

_____

_____

The wall of selfishness becomes a mirror that reflects the tarnished portrait of past personal glories. We see in a glass dimly, as Paul the apostle writes, instead of seeing face to face: "Now we see but a poor reflection as in a mirror; then we shall see face to face. Now I know in part; then I shall know fully, even as I am fully known."[12]

In selfishness we believe we possess the knowledge of good and evil about ourselves. However, the view of self by self is so nearsighted that only a blurry image of who we really are can be perceived.

When I first needed eyeglasses for reading, I could never hold a page far enough from my eyes to get a clearly focused picture. My reach wasn't long enough for me to really grasp what I was reading. Likewise, my selfish grasp is never long enough to reach the deeply embedded aspirations of my inner being. Initially, the fruit I can see, pick, taste, and eat appears to satisfy my inner pangs of spiritual hunger. But once eaten, the fruit of the immediate selfish desire fails to satisfy my deeper quest for meaning, purpose, and direction through life.

Selfishly, Adam and Eve thought that in eating the fruit their hunger to know would be satiated. Instead, just the opposite happened. Shame and embarrassment became the bricks of their wall of selfishness, creating a barrier between themselves and God's presence.

Selfishness exchanges the eternal for the immediate; the invisible for the visible; the lasting for the temporary; and the future for the present. The cry of the selfish is always "I want" instead of "I give."

The moment the wall of selfishness arose between them and God, Adam and Eve felt apart, alone and ashamed. Like ships that had been moored in safe harbor, they now set sail into an uncharted sea without compass, stars, light, or calm. No longer would their lives experience the blessing of, "Go in peace. The presence of the Lord be with you on your way."[13] Instead they would be tossed about continually by waves of doubt, defeat, and discouragement. They would see their children hate each other and their living reduced to barely existing. Instead of eating out of the abundance of a garden, they would toil the earth, working hard to scratch out a meager existence. The price of selfishness would be paid with the currency of loneliness.

In God's presence, I see his face and thereby know my identity—one created in his image.[14] I have purpose and destiny. I can only see myself for what I am now, in all my selfishness. But God sees me for what I can become. I see now. God sees my future: "'For I know the plans I have for you,' says the Lord. 'They are plans for good and not for evil, to give you a future and a hope.'"[15] I grasp only the result, the fruit. But God gives the seed.

For God, who gives seed to the farmer to plant, and later on, good crops to harvest and eat, will give you more and more seed to plant and will make it grow so that you can give away more and more fruit from your harvest.[16]

Selfishly I have

_____

_____

_____

KEYS TO INVITING GOD'S PRESENCE

- Look at yourself in a mirror for ten minutes. Ask yourself these questions:

  - What is my meaning and purpose in life?

  - Did I create me?

  - Is the me I see in the mirror all there is to life?

  - Am I here just for an I-I relationship or do I need an I-Thou relationship?

- List all the significant relationships in your life, those for whom you would give of yourself, those for whom you might even die.

  _____

  _____

  _____

☛ Is God on your list? Are you on his list? Would God give anything or everything for you to be in his presence? Circle how you think God feels about you right now.

Loving   Angry   Pleased

Disappointed   Joyful   Sad

Other _____

☛ God says, "I have loved you with an everlasting love."[17] Can you accept that fact? Go back to the list in the last question and underline how God says he feels about you.

Accepting that another, particularly God, loves me
may be more difficult than loving another.

Abiding Presence

H E D I D N ' T H A V E T O C O M E . W H O ? M Y F R I E N D —
the man whom I had wounded, the one I thought was my
enemy—refused to let my walls of loneliness and selfishness keep him away. My
actions had not altered his feelings toward me. His love was not contingent upon
my behavior. The physical and emotional walls I'd built to keep him away did not
work. My friend came to my door and knocked. He didn't leave just because I
didn't feel like seeing him. He was there for me.

What have you done or said about God? You may have denied his existence or
his presence. You may have cursed his name or others with his name. You may
have abused his creation or his creatures. You may have rejected his words or his
actions. As a result, you may be thinking that finding his presence is impossible.
Not so.

Just like my friend, God came to the garden. He didn't have to come. Knowing
how he had been misquoted, rejected, and disobeyed, God could have stayed
away. He could have destroyed it all and started over. But he didn't.

God's presence never leaves. "He is the One who goes with you. He will not
leave you nor forsake you."[18] We can run and hide, but God is still there. He
comes to meet with us face to face. He draws us into his presence. The walls of
loneliness and selfishness exist, not because they have to remain, because we
permit them to.

What kept the Berlin wall in place? Hostility. Mistrust. Doubt. Fear. Yet the
wall didn't make the people living on either side of it go away. Relatives on both
sides of the wall were still family. Relationships across the wall were waiting for
fulfillment. But someone had to tear down the wall, not just temporarily but permanently. The wall had to come down. And come down it did. Piece by piece
until it was all dismantled.

For years I had publicly and privately degraded the teaching of a well-known television personality. Much to my chagrin, he called me one day. I just knew that I had been *found out!*

"Larry," he asked, "would you fly out to my office and discuss writing a book with me?"

I was mortified. How could I join myself to someone I had demeaned. What if I really came to like him? Even more, what if—dread the thought—I might come to agree with some of his teachings and philosophy.

The only way our estrangement could be bridged would be through a face-to-face encounter. Any excuse not to meet with him would be frightfully lame and inadequate. I began to recognize that my dislike of him might be rooted in my own selfishness and pride. How? Simply this: Admitting that he might be right would be tantamount to confessing that I was wrong. Such selfish pride could keep me from a relationship with him. Such selfishness often keeps me from a deeper level of inviting God's presence.

So I went. We talked. My greatest, selfish fear materialized. He was right. I was wrong. He was gracious. I was selfish. I repented. The book was written; but much more, the friendship took root and grew.

The walls of selfishness and loneliness in your life have not kept God's presence away from you. Rather, the walls have kept you from feeling his touch, seeing his face, hearing his voice, smelling the sweet perfume of his courtship, tasting his goodness, and sensing his presence.

Feeling ashamed? God isn't ashamed of you.

Feeling guilty? God has already forgiven.

Feeling alone? God is there and waiting.

Feeling afraid? God's perfect loves casts out all fear.

Cyril Connolly believed the lie and wrote, "We are all serving a life sentence in the dungeon of self."[19] A room of mirrors appears to have no exit—the way Albert Camus saw life. Likewise, in the garden of beginnings, Adam and Eve stepped behind the walls of selfishness and loneliness. Behind those walls they encountered guilt and shame. Behind those walls they faced banal existence and death. Behind those walls purpose and destiny melted away into the dross of meaninglessness and hopelessness.

Refusing to invite God's presence causes us to exist in colorless, boring bogs of lifeless existence. The walls of loneliness and selfishness are of our design and construction.

What keeps me from dismantling my walls of loneliness and selfishness?

_____

_____

_____

Existence is a room of mirrors, but life can be found in his presence. "God . . . you have made known to me the path of life; you will fill me with joy in your presence, with eternal pleasures at your right hand."[20]

God walks in the cool of the day into your existence. He is present. He desires to meet with you face to face. Why are you hiding? Why are you afraid or ashamed? What lies are you believing?

To tear down the walls of loneliness and selfishness, I must

_____

_____

_____

KEYS TO INVITING GOD'S PRESENCE

⚊ Identify the bricks of shame that you feel. Write them down.

_____

_____

_____

⚊ Now ask God to help you throw those bricks away. Pray a simple prayer: "God, help me throw the bricks of shame and fear away. Take away my bricks of guilt. Thanks."

⚊ You may protest: "It's easy to pray but hard to live this way." How true. Existence is easy. Life is hard. Existence is painless. Life is filled with risk, pain, and hurts. Existence is dull. Life is full. Existence is boring. Life is exciting. Inviting

God's presence will move you from being a victim of existence to a participator in life. Choose life. Find God's presence in living. Write down your conclusion to this sentence: In life, I am finding God's presence to be

_____

_____

_____

God's presence breathes life into the
dead bones of existence.

Tearing Down the Walls of Loneliness and Selfishness

To tear down the wall of loneliness, I must

_____

_____

_____

To tear down the wall of selfishness, I must

_____

_____

_____

To let go of shame, I must ask God to

_____

_____

_____

To let go of guilt, I must ask God to

_____

_____

_____

To move from existence to life, I will

_____

_____

_____

To stop hiding from God's presence, I will

_____

_____

_____

———⚬⚬⚬———

Selfishness walls out the loving presence that offers me
the only hope of conquering loneliness.

Tearing Down the Walls of Anger and Confusion

Can't you see how little time I
have left?
Oh, let me alone that I may have
a little moment of comfort
before I leave for the land of
darkness and the shadow of
death, never to return—
a land as dark as midnight, a
land of the shadow of death
where only confusion reigns,
and where the brightest light is
dark as midnight.

—JOB 10:20-22 (TLB)

Introduction

RAGE PROMPTS PEOPLE TO IRRATIONAL, DESTRUCTIVE ACTS. Road rage provokes an angry, frustrated driver to attack another motorist on a busy freeway. Family rage pushes a father to kill all of his expatriated family. Jealous rage pits brother against brother. Children like Dylan Klebold and Eric Harris, who burst into Columbine High School, blast away with automatic weapons killing students and teachers.

Why? Angry rage. Rage is a killer.

Rage and anger arising from disappointment, frustration, fear, and a host of other inner demons can destroy relationships suddenly. Life is radically altered and shattered by the angry walls we build between ourselves and others, as well as God. Anger keeps us out of God's presence. And anger poisons the potential for a future relationship with God.

Your anger may be triggered by a real or imagined situation. For example, you smoked for years and then developed lung cancer. You might believe God gave you lung cancer to punish you for smoking. Or you held onto a bitter offense against one who used to be a close friend and who is now the most hateful of enemies. Your bitterness ate at your daily outlook until now you face each day as a dark cloud instead of as a bright opportunity filled with possibilities.

Anger at God can be a projection of blame. Something unexplainable or unexpected happens and you blame God. Or someone hurts you, and God gets blamed. For example, a father's sexual abuse toward a child may be the reason for a person's anger at God. They ask, "Why did God allow it to happen?" or "Why did God give me that kind of parent?"

Self-anger distances us from God. When we become angry at ourselves, we have difficulty receiving love and forgiveness from others. God's loving presence never abandons us, but we abandon him. Condemning ourselves, we cannot accept God's love and forgiveness. We cannot find God's presence when our hearts become self critical.

"This then is how we know we belong to the truth, and how we set our hearts at rest in his presence whenever our hearts condemn us. For God is greater than our hearts, and he knows everything."[1]

Have you built a wall of anger between yourself and God? Has something negative happened in your life that has prompted you to blame God? Or has your anger toward yourself or another person cut you off from the desire to find God's presence?

Many of us feel anger toward:

- ➤ Ourselves
- ➤ Our spouses
- ➤ Our children
- ➤ Our boss
- ➤ Our partner
- ➤ People of other races
- ➤ The government
- ➤ Men
- ➤ Women
- ➤ Our parent(s)
- ➤ God
- ➤ Other _____

This anger manifests itself in:

- ➤ Frustration
- ➤ Anxiety
- ➤ Hostility
- ➤ Depression
- ➤ Bitterness
- ➤ Vengefulness
- ➤ Resentment
- ➤ Sarcasm
- ➤ Paranoia

- ➢ Meanness
- ➢ Desire for destruction
- ➢ Desire for evil
- ➢ Other _____

Then there's the wall of confusion. In confusion, we hear many voices, resulting in many thoughts that trample over one another with reckless abandon. Confusion overwhelms us with the inability to communicate clearly with anyone—God, self, or others.

Think of the small amount of confusion created when you try to find a lost set of car keys. You are running late. People are waiting for you. As you rush out the door, you turn to the normal place you put your keys. Empty. Quickly you run to the backup location you sometimes use when laying your keys down absentmindedly. Not there.

Frustrated, you go to the last place you can remember seeing your keys, and still you can't find them. In a state of confusion, you wander aimlessly throughout the house looking everywhere, lifting up each pile of paper, opening every cabinet door, and revisiting every place you've already checked just to see if you have overlooked the hiding place for your keys. An orderly search becomes a confused meandering that leads you nowhere and makes you even later for your engagement.

Confusion arises from a plethora of conflicting messages all vying at the same time and intensity for your attention. Confusion clouds your identity and purpose. Confusion sets you in the wrong direction to do the wrong thing in the wrong way. Confusion renders your communication unintelligible and your purpose unimaginable.

Confusion paralyzes your pursuit of the presence of God. How so? Confusion allows every distraction into your thoughts. You cannot focus or concentrate. You lack the desire to find God's presence because you can't even find yourself.

Feel angry or confused? Unable to find God's presence because of the walls of anger or confusion in your life? This week it's time to tear down these walls.

Destructive Anger

Anger can become murderous. Killing and destruction may not be anger's initial intent, but the end result can be spilt blood. Even though you may be aware of the existence of God's presence, your anger drives you far away from any relationship with God.

Inviting God's presence may require you to tear down numerous walls between you and God. He awaits you just on the other side of your walls. But you must take the initiative. Some walls may be old and resist destruction. You built them. You must tear them down. God will not remove what you insist on maintaining.

Cain's parents had walked in God's presence. They had communed with God. But the walls of shame and guilt, loneliness and selfishness interrupted their intimacy, while distance and separation marked their relationship with God.

The resulting rift between parents and God had been passed along to the children, Cain and Abel. However, some form of communication existed between God and Cain because we read of how they talked to one another after Cain's sacrifice had been made to God.

In this instance, jealous anger erupted within Cain and propelled him to kill his brother Abel. God respected the offering of Abel. Abel gave his best, the first-born of his flock. On the other hand, Cain just gave some grain as an offering to God. He didn't respond with his best. When God didn't respect Cain's offering, Cain became angry and upset. Venting his wrath, Cain killed Abel.

God had warned Cain that his anger would get the best of him if he didn't control it. Uncontrolled anger spews destruction around and within. Unable to control the anger within, Cain erupted with anger and destroyed his brother. His anger killed the person closest to him.

Between Cain and Abel, anger wreaked havoc through murder. Murder isn't just physical killing; it's relational killing as well. "Under the laws of Moses the rule was, 'If you murder, you must die.' But I have added to that rule and tell you that if you are only angry, even in your own home, you are in danger of judgment!"[2]

Anger becomes a murderous wall that leads to the death of relationships and friendships. Such anger breeds both bitterness and contempt between people and between God and me. Standing as a wall between me and God is the one I cannot forgive . . . the one with whom I remain unreconciled . . . the one whom I hate. My venom for that enemy makes me an enemy of God's.

Here's the key to understanding this destructive wall: Anger drives a wedge between people and cuts off relationships. Cain not only cut off Abel through murder, but he built a huge wall between himself and God.

You don't have to be angry with God to put a wall between you and his presence. Anger toward a family member, neighbor, boss, friend, or enemy also separates you from the presence of God.

Consider an electric wire covered by insulation. The wire is filled with power and energy, but you cannot tap into it as long as the insulation covers the wire. Anger is insulating you from the powerful presence of God. You will never tap into it as long as anger surrounds your heart and separates you from him.

Anger grows. With Cain, anger began as jealousy and frustration. God warned him that sinful anger was crouching at the door of his heart. But Cain failed to heed the warning. Left unchecked, anger, like a cancerous tumor, grew in destructive force until it finally destroyed the living relationship between brothers.

Anger becomes a "'black grace.' Such black grace [is] an influx of extraordinary powers, an almost infinite growth of energy, [which] can be observed in angry men."[3] Such an unwanted gift like anger acts like a computer virus that eats away at everything that is orderly in life.

I must remove black grace from my life because

_____

_____

_____

Not only can a present wall of anger keep you from inviting God's presence, but left alone, your anger will grow from a wall into a fortress that imprisons you and keeps out others who would draw close to you. Quickly forgiving and letting go of your anger will release you from the chains of resentment, bitterness, and jealously. "Be angry, and do not sin: do not let the sun go down on your wrath."[4]

Cain bedded down with his anger, fornicated with his bitterness, and soon his jealous wrath gave birth to murderous hatred. His anger drove him from the peaceful presence of God into the tortuous desert of hatred.

Finding God's presence becomes an impossible journey when your soul is trapped in the quagmire of anger.

With whom are you angry? Forget the why. Let go of the offense. Release the lava of inner emotions that erupt into a volcano of wrath as you think about them. Vent the bitterness. Lance the wound and clean the infection out of your system. Holding fast to the object of your wrath prevents you from grasping the object of your affection.

**The following people are those against whom I have carried anger.
I choose to forgive these people.**

_____

_____

_____

KEYS TO INVITING GOD'S PRESENCE

- List what makes you angry. Read the list out loud. Ask yourself whether it's worth the time, energy, and pain of carrying the anger of all this stuff.

- Do a housecleaning of your soul. Like an office filled with junk mail, old papers, and notes that are no longer necessary, the soul can become the trash bin of all your old, angry feelings. Empty the trash bin.

- Make phone calls or write letters or e-mails to those with whom you are still angry. Tell them that you forgive them. Don't rehash the garbage. Refuse to blame or criticize them. Let the letter be your release of pinned-up negative emotions that need to be flushed out of your system forever.

_____

_____

_____

Forgiveness rebuilds a bridge
of friendship first with another
and then with God.

DAY 2

Hiding from God's Face

ANGER MASKS THE FACE OF GOD. REMEMBER THAT being in his presence means to be before his face. Anger clouds the relational atmosphere between you and God. Consequently, his face is hidden from you by the black clouds of anger arising from your inner storms.

In anger, Cain killed Abel. Ignoring the warnings of God, he was driven to find revenge instead of God's presence. Perhaps he was trying to lash out at God with his anger.

My friend, Joseph, did that. His wife died and he blamed God. When asked how she died, he would angrily reply, "God killed her." Of course God did no such thing, but Joseph's perception replaced reality and he believed a lie.

His vengeance took a strange twist. Joseph decided to punish God by not eating. He refused any kind of nourishment. He began starving himself to death. To spite God, he would kill himself to deprive God of the opportunity to slay him. Sick thinking, but that's what happened.

Joseph wasted each day staring out his window in speechless scorn. He frowned at each sunrise and sunset. He despised every breath he took. His bitter anger began to eat away at his body like a terminal disease.

"God is here," I would say when I visited him.

"Can't see him," Joseph would banefully reply.

"Do you want to see him?" I would ask.

"Don't know that I would recognize him if I did," he would sarcastically spit. "And if I did, I wouldn't want to see him anyway."

Joseph's family debated about putting a tube into his stomach to force-feed him. It would have prolonged his existence, but Joseph's hope of life had already vanished. His anger blanketed God's face with an unrecognizable visage. Like a child playing under a blanket tent and having the tent collapse all around him, Joseph found himself enveloped in his blanket of anger and unwilling to climb out. Suffocating in the vacuum of his bitterness, he chose to be hidden from the face of God.

Cain cried out the result of his wall of anger: "I shall be hidden from your face." Instead of pleading for mercy, inviting God's presence, and seeking his face, Cain announced a judgment that God never spoke. He cursed himself.

In the past I have blamed God for a tragedy—either to me or to someone close to me. My anger at that time could be described as:

_____

_____

_____

Anger becomes a self-pronounced curse that hides us from the face of God. Such self-condemnation leaves us lonely and separated. Instead of pursuing God, we run from him. Harboring anger within makes us children of wrath.[5] Inner hostility births a character and personality of anger that poisons every relationship and interaction we have with others. We find ourselves not only cursing others but also ourselves in words and in actions.

Overcoming such wrath requires that we abort anger through admitting it and then releasing it through forgiveness, which often begins with forgiving ourselves. If Cain could have forgiven himself, he would never have cursed himself with being hidden from God's face or presence.

Is God hidden from your sight by the veil of your anger?

Is it impossible to see him through the storm of your hostility toward yourself or another?

If you experience yourself hidden from God, inviting God's presence may need to begin within you as you repent of anger and turn toward forgiveness.

I feel hidden from God's face when

_____

_____

_____

⚷ You may find yourself enveloped in a cloud of anger that prevents you from pursuing God's presence. If you sense such a cloud, describe it.

_____

_____

_____

⚷ Whom do you need to forgive to disperse the cloud of anger? Circle your answer.

- Yourself

- Another person _____

- God

⚷ Remember, you are not forgiving God because he has done anything wrong. Forgiving God is for you, not him. Forgiving God is refusing to blame him for any situation you deem negative or destructive.

⚷ Write a letter to yourself, another person, or God. Describe all that you are angry about. Now tear the letter up or burn it, symbolically releasing your anger and embracing forgiveness.

_____

_____

_____

⊰⊷⊱

Embracing forgiveness invites
God's presence.

Leaving God's Presence

ANGER DRIVES US FROM GOD'S PRESENCE. THE MUR-derous rage that drove Cain to kill Abel also drove him from God's presence: "Then Cain went out from the presence of the Lord and dwelt in the land of Nod on the east of Eden."[6] Yet as angry as Cain was and as hidden as he desired to be from God's presence, God was still there. God was talking with Cain even after the horrific act of murder. God was speaking truth into Cain's life. But Cain couldn't endure the presence of God. He attempted to leave God's presence.

I get angry with God when

_____

I get angry with myself when

_____

The old cliché goes, "You can run, but you can't hide." It may feel as though you have escaped from God's presence, but you haven't. As a young child, you may have put a blanket over your head and pretended no one else was in the room even though a parent was standing right there. The blanket didn't make the parent go away. Your imagination didn't cause the parent to vanish. The blanket merely hid your parent from view. You created the illusion that you had left your parent's presence, but the truth was that your parent hadn't gone anywhere, and you were playing the fool.

Consider this truth:

O Lord, You have searched me and known me.
You know my sitting down and my rising up;
You understand my thought afar off.
You comprehend my path and my lying down,
And are acquainted with all my ways.
For there is not a word on my tongue,
But behold, O Lord, You know it altogether.
You have hedged me behind and before,
And laid Your hand upon me.
Such knowledge is too wonderful for me;
It is high, I cannot attain it.

Where can I go from Your Spirit?
Or where can I flee from Your presence?
If I ascend into heaven, You are there;
If I make my bed in hell, behold, You are there.
If I take the wings of the morning,
And dwell in the uttermost parts of the sea,
Even there Your hand shall lead me,
And Your right hand shall hold me.[7]

Cain ran away from God's presence, but he couldn't reach the boundaries of God because God is boundless. Cain couldn't go beyond God's limits because God is limitless. Finding a place where God does not exist is impossible.

If you have been trying to leave God's presence, ask yourself, "Why?" The reason is rooted in you, not in God. God's presence never left Cain, but Cain tried to go away from God's presence. Perhaps he was driven away by shame, guilt, mistrust, or anger. His rage toward self and God became so great that a separation between Cain and God became Cain's self-imposed exile.

We read that Cain departed to the land called Nod, which literally means "wandering." Nod is that place in your life of restless wandering—always going but never arriving; continual journeys without any destinations; countless goals with no accomplishments; confusing directions without clarity.

Imagine trying to drive a car to a destination blindfolded. You might go in circles or head in the wrong direction. You're moving, but going nowhere. That's the state of a life without seeing God's face, a life trying to depart from his presence. Such existence is Nod.

In Nod we wander from idea to idea, false hope to false hope, theory to theory, and myth to myth. In Nod we discover that what worked for us yesterday fails us today. The best we can do is to continue on, going nowhere and accomplishing nothing.

In Nod we continually try out the answers of others but never uncover any answers for ourselves. Nod holds for us no completions and no destinations. We continually race around a spiral track never crossing a finish line to see a checked flag.

In Nod we wander from person to person, religion to religion, shaman to shaman or psychic to psychic. The more we wander, the angrier we become. The more we wander, the more confused we become.

Wandering cannot lead us to the presence of God. We do not find God's presence by accidentally bumping into it like falling over a chair in an unlit, unfamiliar room.

It's time to stop wandering and to remove the blindfold of anger. Pursuing God's presence isn't a rushing toward something or someplace. Rather, it can simply begin with stopping, being still, and allowing the blindfold to be removed by forgiveness. God bluntly says, "Be still and know that I am God."[8]

When I stop running away and wandering about, I find that God's presence is

_____

_____

_____

KEYS TO INVITING GOD'S PRESENCE

⚷ Pulling down the wall of anger involves admitting to yourself that you're angry. I am angry because

_____

_____

_____

⚷ Pulling down the wall of anger involves choosing to forgive. What if a person has terribly and intentionally hurt you? Forgiving them doesn't excuse them or enable them to escape justice. Forgiveness releases you from having to be their judge, jury, and executioner. Forgiveness also releases you from the burden of continually carrying the pain and hurt. Unforgiveness becomes a cancerous hate that destroys its host. So choosing to forgive heals relationships *and* your soul. Write down the names of those you choose to forgive.

_____

_____

_____

🔑 Pulling down the wall of anger involves coming from behind your wall of anger. God doesn't hide his face from you, but your anger veils his face from your vision. Fill in the following: I will not hide from God's presence when

_____

🔑 Pulling down the wall of anger involves ceasing your wandering. Stop chasing your vengeance. Be still in order to find his presence. "For the Kingdom of God is within you."[9] Fill in the following: I will stop wandering and will start

_____

Stop chasing anger;
chase God's presence.

Ascending to Confusion

THE PURSUIT OF GOD THAT LEADS TO SELF-PROMOTION ends in confusion. The wall of confusion is built by the bricks of misdirection and selfish ambition. Confusion mixes religion and relationship, ritual and righteousness, truth and myth. Confusion is derived from the Latin word *confundere,* meaning "to mix together" or "to mix up and fail to distinguish."

In confusion, we fail to distinguish between God and ourselves. We cannot separate what's essential from what's urgent. We call what is unholy by holy terms and what is sacred by profane terms. We bless curses and curse blessings.

No boundaries or absolutes exist in confusion. Relativism so dilutes truth that one is left with only a quagmire of grays and no definition of right and wrong or light and darkness. Confusion arises out of a lack of purpose and a void of right direction.

The wall of confusion blurs the pursuit of God's presence much like an improper eyeglass prescription confuses the brain and leads the eyes to see blurry images instead of sharp ones. Often well-meaning but misguided friends give us directions toward God that have disastrous results. Religious rituals that worked for them only help to confuse and misguide us. They give us formulas for building a tower toward God that results only in an unstable structure we might label as a house built upon sand. Wisdom builds its structure on a rock that can withstand any wind or storm. But confusion cannot follow the path of wisdom. Instead, confusion is "like a man who builds his house on sand. When the rains and floods come and storm winds beat against his house, it will fall with a mighty crash."[10]

Confusion causes us to listen to competing voices, all claiming to be God but none speaking the truth. "God is not a man, that he should lie."[11] Therefore guiding voices that lie cannot be God. The clearest voice guiding us to God comes from the Spirit itself, not flesh.

In the ancient Hebrew narratives, a story is told of humanity's attempt to reach God by building a tower that would ascend to the heavens. Certainly the desire to find God must be commended. But the method and motive betrayed the end results of such a faulty ascent into God's presence. In a confused state of reasoning, people said to one another, "Come, let us build ourselves a city, and a tower whose top is in the heavens; let us make a name for ourselves."[12] Their thinly guised pursuit of God was actually an ascent to self-promotion.

If your motive in inviting God's presence is rooted in gaining some kind of power, fame, or gain for yourself, then the tower into heaven you seek will simply turn out to be a wall of confusion. Instead of ascending into greatness, you will erect a barrier between yourself and the greatness that is ultimately found in God. "For the Lord your God is God of gods and Lord of lords, the great God, mighty and awesome."[13]

The reason I would invite God's presence in my life is

_____

_____

_____

If you believe inviting God's presence will do something for you, then your marquee of wishful fame will come crashing down in a rubble of confusion. No tower can stand when its internal structure has been compromised. We saw evidence of that when the mighty World Trade Center towers were struck in a dastardly attack of terrorist cowardice. The resulting fireball so weakened the interior steel structure of the towers that they came crashing down. Similarly, any tower we build to reach God's presence in our own strength will lack an internal structure of humility and purity.

We must recognize that God's presence envelopes those with a pure and clean heart stripped of self-seeking motives.

> *Create in me a clean heart, O God,*
> *And renew a steadfast spirit within me.*
> *Do not cast me away from Your presence,*
> *And do not take Your Holy Spirit from me.*[14]

Brother Lawrence reflected:

That practice which is alike the most holy, the most general, and the most needful in the spiritual life is the practice of the Presence of God. It is the schooling of the soul to find its joy in His Divine Companionship, holding with Him at all times and in every moment humble and loving.[15]

When the pursuit of God lacks humility and love, the final destination is confusion, not presence. Trying to find God's presence by building our own spiritual towers, constructed with the effort of selfish motives, fired by the bricks of ego, and cemented with the mortar of pride, will only lead us to a tower called Babel—confusion, bewilderment, and disarray.

I feel confusion in my pursuit of God when

_____

_____

_____

KEYS TO INVITING GOD'S PRESENCE

○⚯ Describe your motives for inviting God's presence.

_____

_____

_____

○⚯ List all the ways others have told you to find God that have failed.

_____

_____

_____

○⚯ When seeking God, do you feel (circle all that apply):

Confused   Perplexed   Bewildered

Lost   Prideful   Self-assured

Other _____

⚬→ Examine your answers. If your pursuit is self-centered or confused, then your destination will be confusion. What will it take to humble yourself in your seeking?

_____

_____

_____

⚬→ Consider the following statement from James the Apostle. Underline actions you will take. Circle actions that are hard for you.

Draw near to God and He will draw near to you. Cleanse your hands, you sinners; and purify your hearts, you double-minded. Lament and mourn and weep! Let your laughter be turned to mourning and your joy to gloom. Humble yourselves in the sight of the Lord, and He will lift you up. [16]

———— ⌘ ————

God's presence promotes those who have no desire for promotion or position.

A Confusion of Words

IN THE TOWER OF BABEL, WE SEE HUMANITY TRYING TO find God in ways that end in disarray. Babel becomes the classic illustration for the wall of confusion.[17] Confused, we lack the ability to communicate with one another or with God. Language becomes a barrier instead of a bridge. Communication is garbled, not clear.

How often I hear sincere seekers of God bemoan, "I am so confused."

They have listened to the words of other self-proclaimed sages who give formula after formula for reaching God. Some teach a karma while others invoke a mantra. Some light candles while others set themselves on fire. Some repeat litanies while others recite poetry. Some wave banners while others wave swords. Some indulge in self-flagellation while others flog the unrepentant. Some sing hymns while others utter ecstasies. Some whisper chants while others shout creeds. Some pray spontaneously while others pray the words in books.

But form never replaces substance, and practice never substitutes for presence.

In building the tower, humanity attempted to ascend to God instead of commune with God. The tower reminds us that the best of human efforts always falls short of touching the outer garment of glorious presence.

In a tower, humanity reached up to God and fell back into confusion. Through a cross, God reached down to humanity and raised up a new creation. The cross replaced the tower, showing us that the way to find God's presence involves replacing pride with humility, replacing promotion with service, and replacing selfishness with sacrifice.

The failure of the tower reminds us that "all fall short of God's glorious ideal."[18]

We would say that a person is confused who tries to build an elevator without a top floor to step onto. Religion continually builds stairs that ascend to nowhere.

Arriving at the top of religion, the climber steps out into nothingness. The result is confusion.

Inviting God's presence is not about religious stair stepping; it's about relationship building. The wall of confusion constructed by religious languages all conversing in a cacophony of words without meaning must be abandoned. Religious words that seek to fully describe, define, and delimit God's presence only confuse the true seeker. The walls of religious terms are barriers between people and between us and God.

Right now my relationships are generally
(put an X on the line to indicate where you are):

Intimate   Distant

Meaningful   Shallow

Peaceful   Tumultuous

Inviting God's presence is not about finding the right words, but rather about knowing the Word. As we tear down the wall of confusion, we will bypass a multitude of words for a relationship with the Word.

At the tower of Babel, humanity's words became so confused that they scattered. At the cross, the Word became so clear that humanity was united with God and unified in his presence.

One of the greatest walls that may obstruct you from inviting God's presence is the wall of religious words and rituals that seem to show the way to him. But God has no interest in our religious towers built of babblings. They merely reduce his presence to a confusing, unapproachable cloud of unknowing.

The confusing words of religious people that I need to discard are

_____

_____

_____

🗝 List all the confusing religious words you have heard over the years that have kept you from inviting God's presence.

_____

_____

_____

🗝 What words does God speak to you that are meaningful and lasting? (Circle all that apply.)

Love   Hope   Faith   Joy   Peace

Patience   Self-control   Truth   Trust

Other _____

🗝 To tear down the wall of confusion, I must

_____

_____

_____

Words inviting God's presence arise from longing and desperation more than from ritual and tradition.

Tearing Down the Walls of Anger and Confusion

To tear down the wall of anger, I must

_____

_____

_____

To tear down the wall of confusion, I must

_____

_____

_____

I need to forgive

_____

_____

_____

I will stop hiding from God's face when

_____

_____

_____

The confusing, religious words I need to let go of are

_____

_____

_____

—⚬⚬⚬—

Anger implodes, rendering me incapable
of being filled by God's Presence.

———⬡⬡⬡———

Tearing Down the Walls of Disappointment and Monotony

We are like sculptors,
constantly carving out of others
the image we long for,
need, love or desire, often
against reality,
against their benefit, and
always, in the end,
a disappointment, because it
does not fit them.

—ANAÏS NIN

Introduction

Passages through life may dampen, discourage, or even derail our pursuit of God's presence. We can become so enmeshed in the busy-ness and routine maintenance of our lifestyles that we put God on a shelf. We only take him off the shelf when we feel the need to use religion as a crutch or crisis management tool.

This week you will examine how going through life can become a distraction to inviting God's presence. It doesn't have to happen but often does when we focus on what's immediate to us. That which is long term and lasting gets put on a back burner and sometimes left there. We don't intend for distractions to keep us from God, but they often do. Identifying and tearing down these walls can keep us on track and on purpose in seeking God's presence.

Israel's ancient history provides us with a pattern for how we experience life's passages. Jacob, later called Israel, went to Egypt with his clan during a famine to find food and live under the protection of his second youngest son, Joseph, who was then Egypt's prime minister. Home for Jacob's family was Canaan, so the journey to Egypt should have been temporary. As happens often in life, what was to be temporary stretched into four centuries. What started as a blessing became a curse of bondage. What began as a family reunion filled with excitement and joy decayed into the monotony of servitude.

This week we will examine some of life's passages against the backdrop of the Israelites' experience in Egypt. Jacob's family discovers life in Egypt wasn't all they expected. Disappointment, along with unfulfilled expectations, became life's daily fare. Life's passages can become walls to inviting God's presence instead of relationships enjoying his presence. Some of the passages this week may not apply to your life at this moment. So read through those most applicable and skim over the others.

Marriage. For too many, the excitement of a marriage beginning with hope and expectations settles into a monotonous, daily routine punctuated with conflicts, problems, and intermittent crises. Intended to be the earthly expression of our spiritual relationship with God, a marriage loaded with unfulfilled expectation and unmet needs too frequently becomes a wall between a spouse and God.

Children. The joy of children too often brings stresses and challenges that tend to pull a couple and family apart instead of producing harmony and togetherness. Expecting the best of our children and ourselves, we often encounter the worst and then lapse into disappointment. We yell rather than discuss. We scream rather than communicate. We punish instead of train. We find ourselves providing our children with a contradictory model of parenthood. They don't see the Father God in us and find themselves abandoned, hurt, and fatherless. Instead of doing and saying what God would have us do and say, we become negative examples. Often our children conclude that if God is anything like their parents, then they don't want anything to do with him.

Home. Searching for a home can be exciting but may also leave us feeling disappointed and frustrated. The home of our dreams may not be affordable. Trying to grasp the dream, we may sink into a bondage of debt that can only be lifted by constant striving. The dream house can become an albatross that drains our finances, consumes our free time with maintenance, and fails to meet our expectations of perfection.

Work. Often with high ideals and hopes, we enter into a career expecting to make it to the top, to impact humanity, to make a name for ourselves, and to provide an inheritance for our children. How often, however, do we enter work out of necessity instead of planning? How often do we find that the initial career isn't the train we want to ride for a lifetime? Mid-life crises and mid-career job changes litter the landscape of families, bringing stress, pain, alienation, and even divorce. Gallup reports that one-third of all workers indicate they would be happier in another job.[1]

Retirement. Some push through the passages of life with blind determination, believing that the goal of life is retirement. But the nest egg is often too small and the unfruitful lifestyle of "playing golf and condo living" produces crabby, cranky, cynical oldsters who rag on the government and live to spend their children's inheritance.

Isn't life meant to be more than successive disappointment and endless monotony? Without the presence of God, existence during life's passages can become simply a process of building one disappointing, monotonous wall after another. This is the week to tear down the walls of disappointment and monotony.

Married but Not Completed?

I OFTEN HEAR SPOUSES SAY:

➤ My mate has no interest in spiritual things.

➤ We never pray or read Scriptures together.

➤ I go to religious services, but my spouse never goes with me.

➤ My spouse is a fanatic about religion. I don't want to be like that.

➤ We're from different religious backgrounds. We don't agree, so we just don't talk about it.

On the other hand, if you and your spouse tear down the spiritual walls between you and God, you can find a fulfilling journey together into God's presence. Some of the spiritual walls that need to come down in marriage before you can pursue God's presence together are:

➤ *Unresolved anger.* Let go of anger quickly. Forgive even before the other person asks.

➤ *Unfulfilled expectations and unmet needs.* Be realistic about expectations. Remember that no one but God can meet all your needs.

➤ *Unhealed hurts.* Ask for what you need. Allow love and mercy to help you forgive past hurts.

➤ *Unkept promises.* Don't promise what you cannot do. When you can't keep a promise, admit it and ask for forgiveness.

➤ *Undignified communication.* Keep your words kind. Stop blaming one another. Take responsibility for your own feelings.

A couple who shares spiritual intimacy models God's relationship with us. It's difficult to be intimate in God's presence when intimacy in marriage is lacking.

Yes, you can find God's presence without your spouse, but it's much more joyful and delightful to seek God together than apart.

For some spouses, their relationship with God is so personal and private that sharing about spiritual things is quite difficult. But sharing isn't limited to just words or even prayers.

Sharing spiritual intimacy can involve:

➢ Going to a house of worship together.

➢ Reading Scriptures or spiritual books together.

➢ Listening to inspirational music together.

➢ Speaking God's blessings over one another.

➢ Listening to and praying for the needs of one another.

I share spiritual intimacy with another person by

_____

_____

_____

Marital intimacy is no guarantee of inviting God's presence, but the lack of intimacy can certainly distract both spouses from their pursuit of God. Seeking God together can draw both spouses closer to one another through:

➢ Learning to love unconditionally

➢ Singing and praising God together

➢ Growing in spiritual knowledge, insight, understanding, and wisdom

➢ Touching one another as you pray for healing and health

➢ Blessing one another with scriptural words

➢ Giving unselfishly to one another

"For this reason a man will leave his father and mother and be united to his wife, and the two will become one flesh."[2] These words, spoken over the first marriage, officiated by God, gives a picture of two people united in the presence of God. The deepest intimacy between humans and God is when a couple in covenant relationship with one another lovingly enter into his presence.

Marital covenant reflects covenant with God. In covenant, we enter into an agreement that is rooted in unconditional love, forgiveness, eternal bonds, mutual protection, and sacrificial provision. In covenant, the Lord unites you to your spouse. In God's wise plan, when you married, the two of you became one in his sight. And what does he want? Godly children from your union. Therefore, guard your passions! Keep faith with the wife of your youth.[3]

Intimacy in marriage can bring both spouses into a deeper and more meaningful experience of God's presence.

In our marriage, our intimacy with God

_____

_____

_____

KEYS FOR INVITING GOD'S PRESENCE

⚷ Circle what actions you are willing to take with your spouse:

- Learning to love unconditionally

- Singing and praising God together

- Growing in spiritual knowledge, insight, understanding, and wisdom

- Touching one another as you pray for healing and health

- Blessing one another with scriptural words

- Giving unselfishly to your spouse at your initiative without even expecting your gift to be reciprocated

⚷ Circle hindrances to intimacy in your marriage:

- *Unresolved anger.* Let go of anger quickly. Forgive one another even before the other person asks.

- *Unfulfilled expectations and unmet needs.* Be realistic about expectations. Remember that no one but God can meet all your needs.

- *Unhealed hurts.* Ask for what you need. Allow love and mercy to help you forgive past hurts.

- *Unkept promises.* Don't promise what you cannot do. When you can't keep a promise, admit it and ask for forgiveness.

- *Undignified communication.* Keep your words kind. Stop blaming one another. Take responsibility for your own feelings.

🔑 What do you need to forgive?

_____

_____

_____

🔑 What pain do you need to be healed of?

_____

_____

_____

🔑 Take time to pray this blessing over your spouse both in your spouse's presence and throughout the day when you are apart. (Replace "you" with your spouse's name.)

> The LORD bless you and keep you;
> The LORD make His face shine upon you,
> And be gracious to you;
> The LORD lift up His countenance upon you,
> And give you peace.[4]

Blessing in marriage helps usher
in God's presence.

DAY 2

Children but Not Harmony?

WHEN CONFLICT AND CRISES ARISE IN PARENTING, A wall can quickly block our pursuit of God's presence. Counseling interviews I have had over the past twenty years suggest that marital happiness plunges to its lowest ebb during the teenage years of childrearing. But of course conflict can arise at any age.

Parenting requires an immense amount of time, work, attention, emotional investment, and financial resources. It's quite a temptation to put God on the shelf when one is so drained after simply handling the daily tasks of parenting. However, without God's presence, parenting can become an impossible burden.

Parenting and inviting God's presence are in conflict when:

➤ *Children are in rebellion.* Rules without relationship foster rebellion. At times, even the most loving parents have children who rebel. Whatever the root of the rebellion, a child in rebellion may distract a parent from inviting or enjoying God's presence.

➤ *Families are in chaos.* Relationship without rules fosters chaos.

➤ *Parents are abusive or reactive.* Parenting requires adults to be loving, kind, consistent in discipline, and proactive.

➤ *Families are independent or codependent instead of interdependent.* A family that constructively supports one another and fosters responsibility provides a stable environment for spiritual growth and maturity for all family members.

➤ *Addiction infects families.* Drug and alcohol addiction or abuse and behavioral addictions such as gambling and sex will turn a family away from God.

- *Materialism becomes the goal of a family.* Materialistic obsession ruins a family's sensitivity to spiritual things.
- *Domination, intimidation, and manipulation invade family relationships.* Controlling and using others destroys trust in a family. Trust is a basic element in the pursuit of God (See Week 1).

On the other hand, parenting and the presence of God can go hand in hand when parents:

- *Model the character of God to their children.* Qualities like love, forgiveness, truth, discipline, loyalty, trust, dependability, creativity reveal his character.
- *Love their children with unconditional love.* Love is patient and kind, never jealous or envious, never boastful or proud, never haughty or selfish or rude. Love does not demand its own way. It is not irritable or touchy. It does not hold grudges and will hardly even notice when others do it wrong. It is never glad about injustice, but rejoices whenever truth wins out. If you love someone, you will be loyal to him no matter what the cost. You will always believe in him, always expect the best of him, and always stand your ground in defending him.[5]
- *Discipline to correct and teach instead of punish and inflict pain.* Proactive discipline sets boundaries with consequences for breaking the rules. It is the best way to guide a child into constructive behaviors and positive attitudes.

Trust between parents models for children the kind of trust we can have toward God who perfectly parents us. Communication that involves listening, dialogue, and respect between parents and children forms an excellent foundation for the communication we have with God called prayer. Blessing—speaking only what God would say and acting only how God would act—conveys that we want our children to succeed and prosper. On the other hand, cursing our children labels them as failures and points them toward destruction.

The words that best describe my relationship with family are

_____

_____

_____

The manner in which you parent reflects the presence of God in your life. As you draw closer to God, you become more like him in the way you treat your family. When you distance yourself from his presence, you put up walls between yourself, God, and your family.

Claiming to be in God's presence and at the same time being cruel or unkind as a parent is the essence of hypocrisy. Religious people who use rules and religious laws to dominate, manipulate, and intimidate family members lack intimacy with a loving, compassionate God.

In the Scriptures, the admonitions for holy parenting exist alongside admonitions to love God:

> *Love the Lord your God with all your heart and with all your soul and with all your strength . . . These commandments that I give you today are to be upon your hearts. Impress them on your children. Talk about them when you sit at home and when you walk along the road, when you lie down and when you get up. Tie them as symbols on your hands and bind them on your foreheads. Write them on the doorframes of your houses and on your gates.[6]*

In Egypt the Israelites were dominated, intimidated, and manipulated by Egypt. But a loving God led that family out of bondage and into freedom—the freedom to be led by God's presence and to love one another.

> *And because he loved your fathers, therefore He chose their descendants after them; and He brought you out of Egypt with His Presence, with His mighty power.[7]*

Loving God leads to loving your children and teaching them about God's presence. Loving your children opens a way for you to move more passionately into the pursuit of God's presence.

My children see God's presence through my

_____

_____

_____

If you are the only portrait of God your family sees, then what does God look like to your family?

_____

_____

_____

How are you showing love to your family? (Circle all that apply.)

Through trust   Through modeling   Through discipline

Through communication   Through blessing

Other _____

If intimidation, domination, or manipulation infect your relationship with your children, what will you do about it?

_____

_____

_____

Parenting mirrors God's presence—
or lack of it.

DAY 3

Settled but Feeling Unsettled?

ONCE THE ISRAELITES LEFT EGYPT AND WERE FREE TO follow God's presence, they discovered life was a journey, not a destination. Even when the Israelites crossed the Jordan and settled in the promised land, life was filled with battles, enemies, conflicts, and danger.

Following God's presence—a pillar of cloud by day and a pillar of fire by night—presented Israel with a unique challenge. The issue of freedom was settled but their dwelling place was not. Life was filled with changes, new experiences, and battles.

People often wishfully say, "When I'm at peace, I will know that I have found God."

Others hope, "If I find the right place to worship and the right people who love God, then I will find God."

However difficult it may be to believe, inviting God's presence is a journey, not a destination, and requires an indwelling of his Spirit, not a physical building. "God, who made the world and everything in it, since he is Lord of heaven and earth, does not dwell in temples made with hands. Nor is He worshipped with men's hands, as though he needed anything, since He gives to all life, breath, and all things."[8]

The only certainty in life is change. God whispers into our sedentary lives, "Behold I'm doing a new thing . . . Do you not perceive it?"[9] *New* implies change. About the time we get settled into one pattern of seeking, pursuing, worshipping, or thinking, God changes us.

The unsettling thing about inviting God's presence is that we can never establish ourselves in one place to put down roots. God continually births something new in our lives.[10] God is always moving ahead of us to a different place, revealing more of himself and his purposes for our lives.

Those who seek God's presence but refuse to change find themselves becoming legalistic and rigid. They refuse to change into new wineskins in order to accept fresh wine.[11] They may become bigoted and prejudiced against anyone or any group whose style of pursuing God differs from theirs.

The feelings I have about change tempt me to

_____

_____

_____

The only constant in life is change. In following God's presence, the Israelites moved from place to place, battle to battle, oasis to oasis, town to town. Their center of worship changed from a tabernacle to a temple and from a temple to the riverbanks of a foreign land. But God was still their focus and the object of their quest so they might know their identity and purpose.

Wilderness, tabernacle, and _sojourner_ are the best words to describe the aspects of pursuing God's presence. You may feel unsettled and disappointed that you haven't yet arrived at a fixed dwelling place of God. About the time you believe you've reached the promised land, the temple may crumple and the promise may move into your future once again. Disappointment may tempt you to build an altar for an idol instead of pitching a tent today, knowing you may have to move on tomorrow.

Many have tried to contain God in a temple instead of within their hearts. The wall of disappointment may begin when we realize that inviting God's presence requires constant change.

As I pursue God's presence in the midst of change, I feel

_____

_____

_____

KEYS TO INVITING GOD'S PRESENCE

⚷ Circle the feelings you have about change:

    Excitement   Fear   Hope   Anticipation

    Dread   Frustration   Anger   Peace

    Turmoil   Anxiety   Worry

    Other _____

⚷ List chronologically the major events of your life. Circle the events that produced the most change in you.

_____

_____

_____

⚷ Think about how God was at work through the changes you have experienced. Read the following Bible verse and think of how it fits with your pursuit of God's presence: "And we know that in all things God works for the good of those who love him, who have been called according to his purpose."[12]

—◦◦◦—

God's presence brings change into our lives.

Working but Not Fulfilled

In a recent movie, I heard an insightful comment: "You do what you are; you're not what you do."

How often have you heard others introduce themselves by their professions?

"Hi, I'm Dr. John Doe," a medical doctor or professor might say.

"Hi, I'm Pastor John," a clergyman might relate.

Or, in answer to the question, "Who are you?" a person might not even give a name but only a job description such as, "I'm a nurse," or "I'm an electrician."

Some people reach midlife unsatisfied with the progress they have made at work or in a career. Some realize they will never climb higher or make more money. Others recognize they are in the wrong job. Others feel trapped in a going-nowhere existence.

Do you find yourself:

➤ Discontent with life or the lifestyle that may have provided you happiness for many years?

➤ Bored with people or activities that have held your interest and perhaps even dominated your life until now?

➤ Feeling adventurous and wanting to experience completely different activities?

➤ Questioning the meaning of life or the validity of decisions clearly and easily made years before?

➤ Confused about who you are or where your life is going?

When I think about my life and accomplishments, I feel

_____

_____

_____

These feelings often are associated with midlife transitions.[13] As you go through the passages of life, you may feel disconnected with what you are doing or where you are going. Anxiety and frustration begin to build the wall of disappointment.

If you believed your career was a divine vocation or "in the will of God," and then later felt disappointed with your work, you might begin to blame God or yourself for your disappointment. Such a wall of disappointment derails your pursuit of God.

Some studies suggest that work is a primary identity factor for many men.[14] Work can certainly drive a wedge into any relationship. Workaholism and work-related stress have weakened many marriages, families, and individual personalities. Additionally, work can produce disappointment and stress that form the bricks and mortar between you and God.

In reality, what you _do_ doesn't determine who you _are_. Your work is simply an extension and expression of your relationships. Work provides income for you and your family. Work gives meaning to certain aspects of your life. But you work to live; you don't live to work.

In many ways, the Israelites' approach to the Promised Land captures for us the challenge of life transitions. The Israelites settled into a routine. They wandered through the wilderness, defeating enemy after enemy along the way. Camp was set up following God's directives. Worship was organized according to God's law. Every aspect of life, it seems, had a protocol.

Upon first approaching the Promised Land, twelve spies were sent to explore the territory. Ten came back fearful and apprehensive: "The land is full of warriors, the people are powerfully built . . . descendants of the ancient race of giants. We felt like grasshoppers before them, they were so tall!"[15] Though two of the spies wanted Israel to invade the land, the disappointing fear of the ten prevailed and the Israelites were doomed to wander in the wilderness for decades.

Your promised land may be filled with disappointment. You have spent your entire career or life to reach this point, but it's not as glorious or promising as you expected. Disappointment fills your life—disappointment about your marriage, children, work, religion, and hobby. What can you do?

God doesn't value you for what you do but rather for who you are. Loving you with an everlasting love, he accepts you for who you are. But a wall of disappointment in yourself, your circumstances, or your relationship can keep you from that promised land filled with the goodness of God's presence.

You have a choice to make: Go forward toward his presence or turn back to disappointment and meaningless wandering.

My greatest disappointments in life up to this point are

_____

_____

_____

KEYS TO INVITING GOD'S PRESENCE

⚷ What disappoints you most about finding God's presence?

_____

_____

_____

⚷ What will it take for you to let go of disappointment and begin to move into God's future for you?

_____

_____

_____

⚷ Decide how you will handle great disappointments.

When I disappoint myself, I will

_____

When I feel disappointed with God, I will

_____

When others disappoint me, I will

_____

When my work disappoints me, I will

_____

🔑 Talk to a friend about your disappointments. Share your feelings. Decide to focus on the possibilities of the future rather than the disappointments of the past.

—— ✺ ——

Pursuing God's presence releases us
from past disappointments.

Monotonous, Not Miraculous?

Miracles, signs, and wonders—how common are they in your life? The miraculous is commonplace in God's presence. The monotonous is commonplace apart from God.

Some protest, "I don't believe in God. I've never seen a miracle or a healing." The truth is those filled with unbelief will never see the miraculous. Or if they do, they will refuse to acknowledge the supernatural can invade the natural.

Israel's bondage in Egypt was filled with monotony. Day in and day out they made bricks and constructed buildings for their taskmasters. Nothing new, exciting, remarkable, or miraculous ever happened. They had forgotten how to believe in a God of miracles and thus had never seen any.

The many routine and monotonous things I do each day include

_____

_____

_____

They dull my sensitivity to God's presence by

_____

_____

_____

Then came a man, one of their own named Moses, who had experienced God's presence and believed that the monotony of slavery could be broken by the God of miracles. Moses didn't find himself seeking after signs, but after the God of signs. Millennia after Moses, another prophet, Jesus, would confirm that those seeking after signs simply would not get them.[16] Why? Signs have no power to convince anyone about the existence of God's presence. Being persuaded to invite God's presence rests in the willingness of the observer to see and understand those signs.

The passionate pursuit of God doesn't arise out of a desire for miracles but rather from a hunger for knowing the Miracle Worker. In inviting God's presence, seek the healer instead of the healing. Expect the miracle worker instead of the miracle. Go after the giver instead of the gifts.

All of the signs God gave the Egyptians didn't persuade them of his presence. The plagues came, but their hearts were not softened toward God. Even the death of all the firstborns of Egypt failed to ultimately convince them that God's presence was mightier than an army of horsemen and chariots.

Interestingly, the Israelites were not convinced of God's presence either, even by the wonderful miracles of the parting of the Red Sea; the provisions of manna, quail, and fresh water; the trembling of a mountain filled with God's presence; and the healing of all sicknesses. They still built a gold calf. They still rebelled against Moses and God. They still refused to follow God's presence into the Promised Land.

The lesson to be learned is this: Miracles may not lead you into his presence, but God's presence is accompanied by miracles, signs, and wonders.

In the monotony of Egyptian slavery, Israel never had the opportunity to experience the miraculous. But when the presence of God was revealed, mighty miracles filled their lives. As you begin to open to God's presence, you will see miracles all around you. What's changed is not God, for he is always at work in miraculous ways. What's changed is your ability to see the invisible and believe the impossible.

In the wilderness, Moses came to a remarkable revelation:

And [God] said, "My Presence will go with you, and I will give you rest." Then [Moses] said to Him, "If Your Presence does not go with us, do not bring us up from here. For how then will it be known that Your people and I have found grace in Your sight, except You go with us?"[17]

The most wondrous experience of my life was

_____

_____

_____

You cannot go forward without his presence. Existence is merely the monotony of slavery without God. His presence sets you free and leads you into the promised land of life: "In Him was life, and that life was the light of men."[18] God is saying to you just as he did to Moses, "My presence will go with you." Allow him to lead you out of monotony and darkness into the life you were purposed to live.

KEYS TO INVITING GOD'S PRESENCE

• Reflect over the last month. Identify all those things you have called luck, coincidence, good fortune, or chance. Circle those events that might be miracles.

_____

_____

_____

• What prevents you from noticing God's presence all around you?

_____

_____

_____

• Talk with a friend who trusts God. Ask that person to share with you the blind spots toward God you may have in your life.

• Do one of the following activities:

  • Tour the newborn nursery of a local hospital.

  • Walk through a forest or along a beach.

  • Listen to inspirational music.

  • Touch the face of a friend or family member.

  • Remember all the random acts of kindness you have experienced recently.

  • Go to a homeless shelter.

  • Pray for God to bless someone else.

- Volunteer for the Red Cross or a hospice.

- Other _____

Then, after fulfilling the activity, ask yourself,
"Where did God's presence go with me?"

*God's presence is at work in
the world around us.*

Tearing Down the Walls of Disappointment and Monotony

To tear down the wall of disappointment, I need to

_____

_____

_____

To tear down the wall of monotony, I need to

_____

_____

_____

For existence to become life for me

_____

_____

_____

I see the miraculous when

_____

_____

_____

I sense God's presence with me when

_____

_____

_____

⸺◦◦◦⸺

Presence provides the lens through which
the miraculous may be seen.

Tearing Down the Walls of Despair and Unknowing

*Despair is the price one pays
for setting oneself an impossible aim.*

—GRAHAM GREENE,
THE HEART OF THE MATTER

Introduction

A SERBIAN FRIEND ONCE SAID TO US, "LIFE IS HARD AND then we die." The difficult circumstances under which she and her family had lived prior to and during the NATO bombing had filled all of them with daily dread and hopelessness.

Despair is the absence of hope. Without God's presence, there is no hope. Thoreau's noted remark still echoes with the ring of reality: "The mass of men live lives of quiet desperation. What is called resignation is confirmed desperation."

Desperation marked the existence of the Israelites when their capital city of Jerusalem was surrounded by the greatest army in the world—the Assryian army of Sennacherib.[1] It was impossible to defeat the army. It was impossible to survive the siege. When existence seems impossible, desperation sets in. King Hezekiah prayed. The people prayed. The nation of Israel was on the verge of extinction. The history of Judaism and indeed the future of Christianity and civilization as we would come to know it hung in the balance. The goal of survival, much less victory, appeared unreachable.

With such an impossible aim, as Graham Greene observes, comes the price of despair: "Losing hope in the pursuit of an impossible aim [goal, purpose, or destiny]" defines despair. Perhaps you have aims, purpose, and a destiny that feel far beyond your reach. Even more, finding God's presence may have seemed impossible. As a result, you have settled into the morass of despair, believing any further pursuit of God is doomed to failure. The Israelites were tempted by this despair, since it would be forty years before the wilderness wanderings would end and once again they could enter into their destiny.[2]

The warning signs of such a wall impeding your pursuit of God are:

➤ *Discouragement when facing giants.* The giants confronting you may be deficit, disease, defeat, or even death. How have these giants hindered your entering into God's presence?

➤ *Delay in achieving your goals.* The frustration that sets in when striving for a goal and not attaining it can be maddening. Is God's presence truly your goal for living?

➤ *Dismay with leadership.* Even those who have been in God's presence—in Israel's case it was Moses—can be inadequate or inferior as leaders from your perspective. When leaders dismay you, how easily do you despair of God's presence?

The fact that we cannot know all there is to know about God tempts us with despair and desperation. The wall of unknowing is built when we are:

➤ *Unable to accept mystery and paradox.* The wall of unknowing is built by our inability to accept mystery or live with paradox. God is good and all-powerful but has allowed for evil and suffering to arise from our freedom to choose. That's sometimes hard to swallow, especially when the suffering and evil touch us or a loved one through death or disease.

➤ *Unwilling to acknowledge holiness.* The wall of unknowing may be built in our response to God's holiness, which is shrouded in *mysterium, tremendum,* and *facinans*—terms we'll discuss later this week. When unknowing fosters doubt and destroys faith we find ourselves lost in the dark of despair. The wall of unknowing tempts us to believe that no path exists to the light and that mystery will leave us forever wandering in a wilderness of despair. However, a path does exist, and we can develop a picture of purpose and destiny even within the unknowing, unfathomable mysteries of God.

This week you will be able to identify and begin to dismantle the walls of despair and unknowing that impede your pursuit of God's presence. Out of God's presence has come a promise to you for this week: "I have made you hear new things from this time, even hidden things, and you did not know them."[3]

Discouraged When Facing Giants

THE GIANTS OF LIFE CAN SO DISTRACT YOU FROM God's presence that you are unable to enter into his presence because you are so busy fearing, fleeing, or fighting them. Giants are those seemingly impossible obstacles that hinder and obscure God's promises and presence in our lives.

Who can easily pursue God when facing the attack of deficit, disease, defeat, or even death in the immediate moment? The wanderings of the Israelites in the wilderness so closely parallel our journeys through the desert of despair that we can learn much from observing their experiences:

The despair of deficit. Any form of lack is debilitating. Israel faced the constant deficit of food and water in the wilderness. Yes, God sent daily manna or bread for sustenance and at times provided meat through quail. But the Israelites still complained. Complaining blinded them to the provisions of God and replaced gratitude with grumbling. "The people were soon complaining about all their misfortunes, and the Lord heard them."[4]

The despair of disease. Disease, whether it attacks us or a loved one, can so drain and debilitate us that we no longer pursue God. We are tempted to give up, quit, blame—ourselves, others, or God—or simply rage at our fate. Moses' sister, Miriam, was so discouraged with Moses' leadership that she complained in the midst of God's presence. God's presence left her and suddenly she became leprous, as white as snow.[5] Her spiritual and physical disease then became a wall between her and God.

Have you allowed your disease, pain, hurt, or suffering to come between you and the living God? Have you distanced yourself from God's presence because you have secretly blamed him for your demise? The despair of disease and lack of a healing can blind us to a vision of God's comforting presence.

The despair of defeat. Failure often haunts us, tearing at our self-esteem and paralyzing us from taking risks. In the wilderness, Israel faced daunting enemies. In one battle (led by Joshua, a mighty general and man of faith) Moses and two friends, Aaron and Hur, overlooked the battlefield. As the friends lifted up Moses' arms in prayer, Israel prevailed. But when Moses and his friends wearied and lowered their arms, the enemy surged forward.[6]

Similarly, you and the friends supporting you can become so fatigued in everyday battles that you risk defeat. A point comes when you reach the end of yourself—your strength, resources, and willpower—to fight on. Without God's presence, waves of despair will crash down, drowning you in failure and defeat.

The despair of death. The ultimate defeat facing you is death. Søren Kierkegaard wrote of the "despair unto death" in which existence loses its meaning and all you have lived to build crumbles. Those in whom you've invested your life desert you. You feel abandoned and alone. You may cry out:

> *My God, My God, why have You forsaken Me?*
> *Why are You so far from helping Me,*
> *And from the words of My groaning?*
> *O My God, I cry in the daytime, but You do not hear;*
> *And in the night season, and am not silent . . . .*
> *I am poured out like water,*
> *And all My bones are out of joint;*
> *My heart is like wax;*
> *It has melted within Me.*
> *My strength is dried up like a potsherd,*
> *And My tongue clings to My jaws;*
> *You have brought Me to the dust of death.*[7]

At the end of yourself, your final cry is one of despair and desperation. You may feel that discouragement has driven you deep into the wilderness of despair from which there is *no exit,* as Jean Paul Sartre bemoaned in his classic work of the same name.

I feel the greatest despair when

_____

_____

_____

Yet in the wilderness we discover the following heartening truths:

God's presence quenches your thirst. Whenever the Israelites found themselves desperate for water, God's presence brought water out of the desert and the rocks. God said to Moses, "Gather the people together, and I will give them water." Then Israel sang this song: "Spring up, O well! All of you sing to it."[8] Nothing will quench your thirst in life's deserts apart from the water that God gives. A promise comes to you that will wash away the grime and dust of despair: "If anyone thirsts, let him come to Me and drink. He who believes in Me, as the Scripture has said, out of his heart will flow rivers of living water."[9]

God's presence satisfies your hunger. In the wilderness, God provided bread to eat as well as water to drink. Daily, God gave manna, which the people baked into bread and ate. Bread is also available to you through God's presence: "Moses did not give you the bread from heaven, but My Father gives you the true bread from heaven. For the bread of God is He who comes down from heaven and gives life to the world."[10]

God's presence overcomes your enemies. God fights your battles and wins your victories. We all reach a point when every resource is depleted, all strength is exhausted, and every human possibility has vanished. When we reach the end of ourselves, we are ready for a miracle and a victory in God's presence. "And the LORD our God delivered him over to us; so we defeated him, his sons, and all his people."[11]

God's presence saves you from death. In God's presence, life overcomes death, blessing obliterates curse, and good defeats evil. "I call heaven and earth as witnesses today against you, that I have set before you life and death, blessing and cursing; therefore choose life, that both you and your descendants may live; that you may love the LORD your God, that you may obey His voice, and that you may cling to Him, for He is your life and the length of your days."[12]

Even as the Israelites faced "giants" upon entering the promised land, we too face our giants—the greatest of which is death. Death attacks us on every front, from physical death to emotional, relational, and intellectual death. Death haunts every curse spoken or invoked against us from persons or the past. But God's presence dispels these giants like the sun melts away the morning fog. Darkness cannot abide light. Cursing cannot overtake blessing. Doubt cannot overcome faith. Death cannot conquer life in His presence.

When facing the wall of discouragement, I

_____

_____

_____

KEYS TO INVITING GOD'S PRESENCE

⚷ Instead of complaining about your giants, make a decision to thank God for all his past goodness and provision in your life. Write down all you have to be thankful for.

_____

_____

_____

⚷ Recognize God as your source and your strength. Read the following verses aloud daily and let God's presence speak to you through the words:

> The LORD is my light and my salvation;
> Whom shall I fear?
> The LORD is the strength of my life;
> Of whom shall I be afraid? . . .
> For in the time of trouble He shall hide me in His pavilion;
> In the secret place of His tabernacle He shall hide me;
> He shall set me high upon a rock . . .
> When You said, "Seek My face,"
> My heart said to You, "Your face, LORD, I will seek."[13]

———⊶⊷———

God's presence quenches your thirst.

Delayed from Achieving Your Goals

IMPATIENCE GIVES RISE TO FRUSTRATION AND ANGER when you reach for a goal only to be thwarted. Sometimes your goals are diametrically opposed to the pursuit of God. But even if your goals are pure and on-purpose with God's destiny for you, how well do you handle waiting?

For hours people waited in New York City to register their missing loved ones after the World Trade Center tragedy. They waited patiently because delay was understandable and related to the most important priority in their lives—the fate of a loved one. It was their sole priority.

Likewise, the critical question for you at this juncture in your journey must be this: Is inviting God's presence simply a goal or my life's priority? If inviting his presence is a goal among many, you will have a rude awakening. God refuses to sit atop your priority list. In fact, he doesn't want to be on your list. As a jealous God, he desires your full, undivided attention and loyalty.

For me God's presence is a

_____

_____

_____

Many people merely list God as a part of their daily to-do list:

➤ Talk to God.

➤ Kiss my spouse.

➢ Hug the kids.

➢ Work hard.

➢ Enjoy my time off.

➢ Eat and exercise.

➢ Get enough rest.

Delays interrupt and punctuate our pursuit of his presence because we allow our idols to compete with his presence as though he were also an idol. But God is clear about his commandment on all of our lives:

"You shall not make for yourself a carved image, or any likeness of anything that is in heaven above, or that is in the earth beneath, or that is in the water under the earth; you shall not bow down to them nor serve them. For I, the Lord your God, am a jealous God."[14]

God needs to *be* your list. He is the only priority. He doesn't ask to be included with all your other important, urgent, and essential activities. He will not share honor, glory, attention, or priority with anyone or anything else.

"So how do I pursue God's presence and find time for anything else?" you may ask.

Good question.

Simple answer.

Instead of thinking in categories or compartments, think holistically. "Hallowed be thy name, thy kingdom come, thy will be done, on earth as it is in heaven," we pray. If we don't pursue God's presence in all that we do, we will never find him in anything that we do. We must seek his presence in every relationship, every activity, every event of life. We must find his presence in our marriages, families, parenting, jobs, and hobbies. In other words, we must allow God's presence to permeate everything.

To pursue God's presence apart from all that we do and say makes our pursuit idolatrous. Such a pursuit so compartmentalizes God that we never allow him to touch, alter, or change any relationship or activity. Instead of saying, "I will go to work and then go to church to worship God," we must begin to say in inviting his presence:

➢ I go to work with God.

➢ I go to church with God.

➢ I go home with God.

➢ I enjoy playing with God.

When inviting God's presence is your life's goal, then in his presence all your needs are met, your priorities are ordered, and your goals are directed.

When delays enter my life, I discover that

_____

_____

_____

KEYS TO INVITING GOD'S PRESENCE

List all the priorities of your life. Is God on the list, Lord of the list, or simply absent from all priority?

_____

_____

_____

Describe those people, things, or events that delay you from making God your life's priority.

_____

_____

_____

In order to seek his presence, what idols must you shatter?

_____

_____

_____

Inviting God's presence must become your life's priority.

DAY 3

Dismayed with Leadership

"IF THAT'S THE WAY GODLY PEOPLE ARE, THEN I WANT nothing to do with God," my friend protested. The fall and immoral transgressions of leaders can often hinder our pursuit of God. Trying to experience God vicariously through them, we elevate them to such heights that when they fall, we angrily dismiss them and the God they serve from our lives.

The Swaggarts, Bakkers, and the local pastor who ran off with a church member can all dissuade us from seeking God. However, they are not the locus of our pursuit or the reason for desiring God's presence. Yes, they may have reflected a godly presence in something they said or did, but like the moon, they are only the reflection and not the source of light.

Time and time again, the people of God saw human failings and foibles in Moses. They recognized that God's presence, although upon him, was not incarnate in him. Moses was not the Presence.

And the LORD went before them by day in a pillar of cloud to lead the way, and by night in a pillar of fire to give them light, so as to go by day and night. He did not take away the pillar of cloud by day or the pillar of fire by night from before the people.[15]

Sam Hinn often comments, "We are never changed in the presence of a man. We are only changed in God's presence." Only God's presence has the power to create, move, change, fill, empower, and guide us. But . . . he uses leaders to teach, equip, and inspire people to seek his presence.

Traits that dismay us about leadership include:

➤ *Hypocrisy.* The walk doesn't line up with the talk, and the character of the leader lacks integrity.

- ➤ *Hyperbole*. The leader exaggerates both his own abilities and the gifts of other leaders.

- ➤ *Pride*. The leader has an ego that gets in the way of her witness to God's presence.

- ➤ *Foolishness*. A leader says foolish words and acts in foolish ways, lacking wisdom and common sense.

My own negative trait that dismays me the most is

_____

_____

_____

No human leader can be a perfect guide into God's presence. Furthermore, imitating and vicariously seeking God's presence through the life of another person robs us of intimacy and closeness with God. Mentors and role models are wonderful teachers but no substitute for his presence.

Moses himself is a prime example of a wonderful spiritual leader who himself failed to reach the Promised Land due to a fit of anger. In angry disobedience, Moses, the man who radiated the presence of God, struck a rock to get water for the complaining Hebrews and found himself distanced from God's presence, not to mention forced to experience the consequence of being deprived of leading Israel into Canaan.

As a spiritual leader, Moses recognized his own limitation and inadequacies in leading the Hebrews into Egypt. He readily confessed to God, "If your presence does not go with us, do not bring us up from here."[16]

Spiritual leaders and mentors reflect God's presence but are not channels for a special experience of God that you cannot receive yourself. No one is needed to experience God for you. Just like Adam and Moses, you can come into God's presence and meet him face to face.

Don't let a leader so disappoint and dismay you that God's face is hidden from you. Move beyond any offense you have with a spiritual leader and into God's presence. Don't judge all spiritual leaders by a few fallen ones. The leader most able to help you find God's presence is the one most willing to serve, to humble himself, to admit that she does not have all the answers. That kind of leader will possess a passion for God's presence.

Make this promise your hope:

For I know the thoughts that I think toward you, says the Lord, thoughts of peace and not of evil, to give you a future and a hope. Then you will call upon Me and go and pray to Me, and I will listen to you. And you will seek Me and find Me, when you search for Me with all your heart.[17]

Three good plans I have made that have positively impacted my life are

_____

_____

_____

Three good plans that I will invite God to birth into my future are

_____

_____

_____

KEYS TO INVITING GOD'S PRESENCE

⚷ Write a prayer thanking God for each person from your past who has positively mentored, taught, or discipled you.

_____

_____

_____

⚷ Seek out a spiritual mentor or leader who has integrity, moral character, and closeness to God's presence. These are the spiritual qualities most needed in a leader: "But the fruit of the Spirit is love, joy, peace, longsuffering, kindness, goodness, faithfulness, gentleness, self-control."[18]

⚷ Think about some spiritual leaders who have dismayed or offended you. Write a prayer forgiving them.

_____

_____

_____

Inviting God's presence does not depend on the leadership of others.

Unable to Accept Mystery or Paradox

HOW DOES A FINITE MIND WRAP ITSELF AROUND that which is infinite?

How does a body limited by time and space understand a spirit living in eternity?

How does limited knowledge and understanding comprehend infinite wisdom?

A popular TV commercial pictures a foolish man who has rented a car from a second-rate rental car company. When questioned by his colleague if the inferior company measures up to the customer service standards of the best company, the foolish man has to admit, "Not exactly."

Do we understand the whole nature of God? Not exactly.

Is truth always fathomable? Not exactly.

Can we perfectly understand God's will for us? Not exactly.

When we find our walls torn down and enter into his presence, will everything go peacefully and perfectly? Not exactly.

Legalists have every problem solved and every question answered and neatly packaged for quick consumption. But Israel wandered in a wilderness for forty years without God answering every question or explaining every mystery of the universe. During their wilderness journey, God made a curious demand of the people who followed his presence: "Be holy, for I am holy."[19] How is that possible? How can flesh be like God? It's only possible when his presence surrounds and indwells us.

Now, if you seek his presence with the ulterior motive of finding an answer to every question, you will be sorely disappointed. While God often gives answers, his thoughts and ways are far more mysterious than we would like to admit. But we need more than answers, you may be thinking. We need presence. But to enter his presence, we must be holy.

Rudolf Otto writes in *The Idea of the Holy* that holiness consists of three elements—*mysterium, tremendum* and *facinans:*

Mysterium refers to the unanswerable mystery that is God. If we are to be holy, we must be willing to accept mystery. Mystery allows for some questions to go unanswered, some problems to go unsolved, some paradoxes to remain in place, and some dilemmas to go unresolved. The wisdom literature declares:

> *Can you fathom the mysteries of God?*
> *Can you probe the limits of the Almighty?*
> *They are higher than the heavens—what can you do?*
> *They are deeper than the depths of the grave—what can you know?*
> *Their measure is longer than the earth*
> *and wider than the sea.*[20]

Tremendum refers to our fear and awe of God. To think that we can enter his presence without a holy fear is to be naïve. The Israelites came to a mountain cloaked in his presence only to rush away in fear and trembling. He is a mighty God and he demands our awe, worship, and reverence. "You shall walk after the Lord your God and fear Him, and keep His commandments and obey His voice; you shall serve Him and hold fast to Him."[21]

Fascinans refers to that which attracts us to God. God woos us with his love as a bridegroom woos his bride. He intrigues us with his beauty and holiness. He offers us every good and perfect gift. We are fascinated by the infinite God who longs for us to be in his presence. Again we are reminded that he says, "I have loved you with an everlasting love."[22]

To be holy as God is holy is to accept mystery and paradox, to reverence and fear him, and to be drawn close to him in an intimate relationship. Knowing God is never a mental exercise to prove his existence from an ontological, teleological or cosmological perspective. Knowing God is always about intimacy. Inviting God's presence never discounts the intellect, but it always engages the heart.

Being holy is to be willing to be made pure in God's presence. Accepting us where we are, he never allows us to stay there. He loves us too much not to change us to be more like him. And that change involves becoming holy—set apart, consecrated, pure—and dedicated totally to an intimate relationship with him.

I am unable to accept mystery and paradox when

_____

_____

_____

KEYS TO INVITING GOD'S PRESENCE

⚷ List two or three mysterious things about God that most confound you.

_____

_____

_____

⚷ Are you willing to pursue his presence even if you do not get the answers about God that you want? Explain.

_____

_____

_____

⚷ Complete these sentences.

I fear God when

_____

I reverence God because

_____

I'm in awe that God

_____

I am drawn to God because

_____

When you cannot get all the answers you want to the questions you have about God, what do you do?

_____

_____

_____

Holiness is found in God's presence.

Unwilling to Be Holy

As I reminded you yesterday, God has made a demand of you: "Be holy as I am holy." Holiness isn't making yourself a religious fanatic. Holiness isn't your ability to purify yourself. Only God can forgive and cleanse you. Holiness isn't wearing certain clothes, following particular customs, or reciting prescribed rituals. Holy people may in fact do such things, but their doing them doesn't make them holy.

What makes us holy is being in the presence of a holy God. We have been set apart for God's exclusive use. "And you shall be holy to Me, for I the Lord am holy, and have separated you from the peoples, that you should be Mine."[23]

Unholy people try to stay in control. They possess themselves and wish to own and control others. Controlling people have difficulty yielding to God's presence or to another person when that person's actions or words are antithetical to their own. Holy people surrender control to God. Surrendered people don't feel the need to rescue or smother others with their beliefs or emotions. Instead of trying to possess their mates or children, they release them and others to God. Holy people understand that all relationships and materials in life are gifts of grace, not possessions to be managed or controlled.

Unholy people possess things and try to own them. In possessing things, they believe that they have increased their merit and worth in the eyes of God and others. Holy people are possessed by a passionate love for God. Their concern isn't in what they possess but in what possesses them—love.

Unholy people use people and love things, surrendering to manipulation and idolatry. Holy people surrender to God. In that surrender everything idolatrous is shattered and God alone worshipped.

Unholy people try to sacrifice things so God will be appeased and thus regard them as holy. Holy people are living sacrifices dedicating themselves wholly to God. They have become both the altar and the sacrificial offering to be consumed by the fire of God's presence.

Unholy people seek to earn God's acceptance. Unholy striving focuses on *trying*. Holy people realize they can never earn God's grace so they accept God's mercy as a free gift. Holiness focuses on *trusting*.

Unholy people regard themselves and certain things as holy. Holy people know that only God is holy. He alone makes holy whoever is in his presence.

Unholy people try to separate the sacred from the profane, taking it upon themselves to label what they regard as holy and unholy. Holy people recognize all that is created by God as holy unto him and understand that only God knows the holy.

Unholy people have difficulty accepting anyone less holy than themselves. Holy people understand that it is only through God's mercy that they have received acceptance and favor. God alone can accept that which is unholy and make it holy. Unholy people act and speak truthfully when it's convenient. Holy people live truth even when it's inconvenient or uncomfortable.

I am most uncomfortable with truth when

_____

_____

_____

I love the truth when

_____

_____

_____

Unholy people exist for the moment. Holy people dedicate each moment as a sacrament, a sacred moment, to God who transforms the temporal into the eternal by his word and power.

Unholy people introduce darkness into ideas, morality, and relationships. Holy people are light in the darkness.

Unholy people use whatever means available to accomplish their ends. Holy people are used by God in whatever way he chooses to accomplish his ends.

Unholy people are past driven, policy driven, people driven, or purpose driven but fall short of being holy. Holy people are Presence driven. The wind of God's presence fills the sails of their lives. Instead of rowing, they are sailing. Instead of idly sitting by, they hoist their sail ready to catch the wind of God's presence whenever and wherever it blows.

Unholy people cannot live with the mystery of unknowing or with the paradox of being known by God while not fully knowing him. Holy people accept mystery and allow themselves to be known fully even when they cannot know God fully.

Unholy people build a wall between themselves and God. Holy people build a wall between themselves and all that would separate them from God.

I am unholy when I

_____

_____

_____

KEYS TO INVITING GOD'S PRESENCE

🔑 Describe a situation or relationship in which you find yourself right now that you know makes you unclean, impure and unholy.

_____

_____

_____

🔑 Listen to God's presence. Invite God's presence to tell you how you can separate yourself from this situation or relationship that is unholy. What are you hearing?

_____

_____

_____

🔑 Quietly ask God to make you holy. Listen to what he speaks to you. Write it down.

_____

_____

_____

⚬∞∞⚬

Being unholy separates us
from his presence.

Tearing Down the Walls of Despair and Unknowing

I despair when

_____

_____

_____

I am hopeful because

_____

_____

_____

I am desperate for

_____

_____

_____

God has made me holy for

_____

_____

_____

I am willing to live with the mystery of

_____

_____

_____

The wall of unknowing can only be torn down through

_____

_____

_____

I am drawn to God when

_____

_____

_____

Facing the impossible with God, I can

_____

_____

_____

———⦵———

Presence imparts the holy.

Tearing Down the Walls of Mere Existence and Pain

Of course God is the 'wholly other';
But He is also the wholly Same,
*   the wholly Present.*
Of course He is the Mysterium
*   Tremendus that appears and*
*   overthrows;*
But He is also the mystery of the
*   self-evident,*
Nearer to me than my I.

> —MARTIN BUBER,
> *I AND THOU*

Introduction

YOU HAVE A CHOICE BETWEEN LIFE AND EXISTENCE. THE question you face immediately is not, "Is there life after death?" Rather, you must face the question, "Is there life after birth?"

We are not talking about eating, breathing, walking, and talking as life. We are speaking of life as being an abundant, meaningful, and prosperous time for you to move beyond the routine to the charged excitement of finding God's presence. His presence transforms existence into life. Existence is the state in which the Israelites found themselves after Joshua led them in conquest of Canaan. After most of the cities were conquered and most of the enemies defeated, the Israelites settled down into a humdrum existence that was simply a cycle of uneasy periods of peace followed by painful war, turmoil, and bondage.[1]

The Israelites' experience with existence may closely parallel yours. The Israelites wandered many places, always following after God's presence but never really close to him. They had feasts, priests, sacrificial practices, and ritual to get somewhat close, but not really intimate, with God. Moses, the priests, and Joshua came closer to God's presence, but Israel always followed and watched the cloud of God's presence from afar. Intermediaries were always necessary to approach him.

Once the Israelites had crossed the Jordan River and battled through some of the towns of Canaan, they quickly settled down to an agrarian lifestyle even though they knew nothing about farming. Instead of listening to God for purpose, direction, and meaning in life, they began to listen to their farming neighbors—the Canaanites from whom they not only learned about farming but also learned about idolatry. They were sojourners, wanderers, tribal people. They experienced few victories and regular setbacks as their enemies, the Philistines, harassed them, attacked them, stole their crops, and often enslaved them like the Egyptians of old.

What does the wall of mere existence look like?

Busy routine without purpose. There was a routine and rhythm to the Israelites' days, but the pursuit of God was replaced with static idols from the existing Philistine culture. Our experience is similar. Instead of allowing the pursuit of God to fill our days with meaning and purpose, we find ourselves mesmerized by the cultural idols of TV, movies, music, sports, and entertainment that, once experienced, leave us empty. In our busy existences, we don't have time for inviting God's presence.

Maintenance without progress. In the life of mere existence, we have so much to maintain: houses, cars, credit, status, equipment, electronics, computers. By the time the oil is changed, the policies renewed, the bills paid, and the plumbing fixed, we collapse exhausted into bed without having accomplished one new thing, even though, as I said before, God constantly reminds us: "See! I am doing a new thing! Now it springs up; do you not perceive it?" Life more closely resembles a carousel than a victorious march into eternity.

Time passing but wasted. We spend a lot of time staying busy but doing nothing of lasting importance. We accumulate treasures that have no enduring value. Laying up treasures for ourselves that moths can eat and rust can destroy, we discover the ephemeral nature of "stuff" and the fickle whims of relationships. Gossip, rumor, chat rooms, and e-mails fill our time, with little or no impact relevant to the real meaning of life.

The Israelites' wall of existence—during a period of her history before the monarchies—was characterized by these defining statements. Merely existing, they:

➢ Did what was right in their own eyes

➢ Did not remember the Lord their God

➢ Failed to show gratitude

➢ Pursued evil instead of good

➢ Worshipped gods instead of God

Another passage in Israel's history was the painful period of the kings. While there were moments of glory with David and Solomon, the monarchy after a few generations crumbled into a divided kingdom with first the northern kingdom and then the southern kingdom being conquered and led off into exile.

Suffering the pain of division and the loss of identity, Israel lost her way in pursuing God's presence. Suffering became an ongoing saga for the people who had once pursued God's presence. They replaced God's presence with a king and replaced the dynamic tabernacle worship with temple ritualism. In the end, the kings were killed, the temple was destroyed, and the people were scattered over the face of the earth. Pain and suffering became the wall between itself and God.

The walls of existence and pain so distract us from God's presence that we become preoccupied with survival and the pursuit of pain relief. We become numbed through the use of medications, drugs, and cultural anesthetics such as TV, entertainment, recreation, and amusements. Instead of living in God's kingdom, we spend our money and our time at the Magic Kingdom. Instead of spiritual warring through faith and prayer, we are content to watch *Star Wars*. Numbing existence and pain render us unable to see the cloud, feel God's touch, or experience the awe of his presence.

It is time to move from a mindless, senseless, emotionless existence—behind the wall of numbing pain—to continue the pursuit of God's presence.

DAY 1

Busy Routine without Purpose

CONSIDER THE ROUTINE OF YOUR DAILY EXISTENCE. Existence is characterized by routine, but becomes insanity when we expect different results even though we keep doing the same things the same old ways.

Existence is purposeless. Existence births ennui. Ennui births escapism. And escapism births extinction. Life, on the other hand, is purposeful. Purpose is always birthed by God's presence. Presence births a plethora of plans so that when one misfires another burst forth to ignite. Plans birth prosperity and productivity so that every plan that's a "God idea" becomes fruitful. All fruit contains substance to sustain and seed to sow into the future.

Existence defines the present by the past. All that existence has to look forward to is tradition and ritual—repeating the way things were instead of anticipating the way things might become. Life impregnates the present with the future. Excitement and enthusiasm fills life with hope and expectancy that the future will be overflowing with change, freshness, and newness. Life embraces change and confidently invites the new.

Existence maintains. Existence becomes preoccupied with corrosion and erosion. Existence is filled with worrying about what's wasting away and cannot be replaced. Life creates. As the old passes away, life builds something new and inventive. In life, invention replaces convention and reformation conquers conformation.

Existence preserves the old. Existence resists what's new, fearing that all may be lost when the new arrives. Life celebrates the new. While learning from and giving thanks for the benefits of the old, life uses the old as a foundation for the new instead of allowing the old to imprison the new.

Existence slowly runs down and out of energy, ending in death. Life recharges us with vitality, ending in resurrection.

Existence becomes mired in misery. Pain and hurt become the only religious acts known in existence. Life overcomes misery. Hope is birthed in the redemptive suffering that bring healing instead of pain and forgiveness instead of hurtful vengeance.

Existence scratches for a little happiness. Existence can only believe in and react to what is. Existence can only hear the credible, see the visible, and do the possible. Why? Because the voice of presence has been silenced, the vision of presence has been darkened, and the possibilities of presence have been denied. Life overflows with joy. Life puts forth a joyful faith that hears the incredible, sees the invisible, and does the impossible because Presence indwells all of life.

The things that make me feel happy and fulfilled are

_____

_____

_____

Existence builds a wall between us and God. Life pursues God, opening doors to his presence.

Existence is blind to miracles. Life is filled with the miraculous.

Are you just existing or are you living?

As the Israelites settled in Canaan after the conquests, their lives filled with agrarian routines like sowing, tending crops, and reaping. At times their enemies, the Philistines, would attack and steal their crops, but they simply rebuilt their homes and lives. Soon forgotten was the wilderness journey in which the Israelites made the effort to worship God at the tabernacle and to follow the cloud of God's presence.

Pursuing God's presence takes time, work, and determination. God demands our full attention. Blessing comes to those who seek him wholeheartedly.[2] That means complete attention without being distracted by routines and busy-ness.

Have you ever tried to have a conversation with someone and watch TV at the same time? The other person knows you aren't giving your full attention. Communication on such a level more often misses the mark than connects with the other person. If our heart is more focused on issues other than God, then we haven't given our full attention to him.

What keeps me so busy that I'm distracted from pursuing God?

_____

_____

_____

KEYS TO INVITING GOD'S PRESENCE

🔑 I'm just existing when I

_____

_____

_____

🔑 Set aside time today to think upon the nature and presence of God. Meditate on God's goodness to you. List all the ways that life is full and meaningful.

_____

_____

_____

🔑 Describe what most hinders you from encountering God's presence in a worship service or church meeting.

_____

_____

_____

God's presence transforms
existence into life.

Maintaining, but Not Progressing

TREADING WATER. IT'S A COMMON EXERCISE IN A pool when you're in the deep end and the water is over your head. Treading water is an exercise in going nowhere and encountering nothing new.

Finding God's presence cannot be like treading water.

Progress always moves you from the present into the future. Regression points you back to what you have left. Treading water does serve a limited, useful purpose. You grow stronger. You develop patience. You keep breathing. But the future never invades your present with the transforming power of newness, freshness, and discovery. Your entire attention is on maintaining.

Let me ask you: "How is your relationship with God progressing? Are you going anywhere with him?" Maintaining what you have experienced gives you a witness but never moves you into a living relationship. You can testify to what God has done but you never discover what God is doing.

Ask yourself:

➤ What is God doing in my life now?

➤ Where is God leading me?

➤ What is God doing in the lives of those around me?

➤ If someone I know is progressing into God's presence, why don't I join them?

Imagine yourself with plates spinning atop tall, slender sticks like a circus performer. You must keep all the plates spinning. The same is true of your life; you must keep spinning the plates you have atop your sticks. You have a significant problem: As long as you maintain your current spinning plates, you are unable to add any new plates.

To add new plates, you must stop spinning an old one. You must let go of something old to add something new.

What am I maintaining that I should let go of in order to move ahead in finding God's presence?

_____

_____

_____

Finding God's presence is a journey, not a destination. You must progress into the future. Maintenance requires hard work but involves little risk. Progress requires both hard work and much risk. Are you willing to become a risk-taker?

Finding God's presence requires you to become open to change. That's difficult if you are stuck in a maintenance mode. Maintenance is comfortable, filled with routine, filled with the predictable. But God loves you too much to leave you the way you are. As you begin finding God's presence all around you, you and circumstances will both change. The question is whether you will allow that change or resist it?

Being stuck in the present dooms you to living in the past. You cannot grow as a person or in relationships without moving forward. Finding God's presence pushes you into the future. The process is about moving from where you are to where he is. He's ahead of you as well as with you. He's in your future as well as in your present. Get ready for change!

As soon as the Israelites tried to settle down in the Promised Land and become comfortable, they faced continual enemies, battles, and trials. In order to move forward, the Israelites crowned a king—first Saul, then David, and finally Solomon. Israel's kings transformed the nation from a simple farming culture to one of the strongest military kingdoms and richest empires of the day.

Two important things happened: Progress invited God's presence in the worship at the Temple. Progress also invited enculturation. Israel began to make their worship a part of the state religion instead of separate and holy. As long as Solomon kept Israel's focus on worshipping God in His holy Temple, God's presence filled the house and the people. But the moment Solomon began to build temples to other gods, the people were blinded to Presence. The key then to inviting God's presence became the exclusive and lavish worship of the living God unadulterated by the worship of any other gods.

The Israelites moved from worshipping in a tent to building one of the wonders of the ancient world—Solomon's temple. And the result of that progress was described and defined by the presence of God: "And it came to pass, when the priests came out of the holy place, that the cloud filled the house of the LORD, so that the priests could not continue ministering because of the cloud; for the glory of the LORD filled the house of the LORD."[3] The temple became the focus of lavishing worship on God and the focus of God lavishing his presence on his people.

What needs to change in my life so I can move forward in worshipping God lavishly?

_____

_____

_____

KEYS TO INVITING GOD'S PRESENCE

⚷ Describe ways you have made progress in finding and inviting God's presence into your life since you began this journal.

_____

_____

_____

⚷ How do you find yourself lavishing God with worship? (Circle all that apply.)

Through corporate worship with a gathering of people.

Through inspirational music.

Through the awe and wonder of creation.

Through Scripture or devotional material.

Through prayer.

Through _____

⚷ List changes you need to make to progress further in your pursuit of God's presence.

_____

_____

_____

⸎

Finding God's presence moves us forward
and changes us eternally.

Wasting Time

O NE OF THE GREATEST BRICKS IN THE WALL OF existence between you and God's presence is wasted time. Whenever time passes without meaningful communication between you and God, that time has been wasted.

What is time about? Loving God and loving others wholeheartedly. "You shall love the LORD your God with all your heart, with all your soul, and with all your mind . . . . You shall love your neighbor as yourself."[4]

The absence of loving God wholeheartedly becomes a wall between us and God's presence. Love takes time. Time devoted to talking. Time devoted to sharing. Time spent with God. But time-robbers and time-wasters erode our relationships and distance us from God.

The time-wasters that most regularly haunt me—from least to most frequent—are

_____

_____

_____

Time-wasters may bring momentary pleasure, but they fail to make an enduring difference. Some of them, such as television, the telephone, and your job, can be very valuable and necessary in your schedule. The question to ask yourself is this: "Is what I'm doing right now going to contribute to my eternity?"

Time spent in God's presence fills our moments with lasting memories of love, joy, peace, and grace. Such moments in God's presence build a foundation for the future, project hope, and fill relationships with intimacy.

How can you redeem your time while enjoying God's presence? "Walk in wisdom toward those who are outside, redeeming the time. Let your speech always be with grace, seasoned with salt, that you may know how you ought to answer each one."[5] Enjoying God's presence and redeeming your time, means that you will:

➤ Be loving, encouraging, and affirming family members

➤ Offer spontaneous acts of kindness

➤ Be gracious and gentle with strangers

➤ Find ways to serve others

➤ Sing songs that inspire and uplift

➤ Say words that exhort and encourage people

➤ Give hugs, shake hands, squeeze shoulders, and pat the backs of others

Remember: Entering God's presence isn't about being religious; it's about being in relationship with him. Rules tend to discourage entering God's presence. They demand that you be righteous and holy before entering his presence. But if you have to wait until everything is right, then you will waste time earning grace that cannot be earned and trying to deserve his presence when no one is worthy of it. We are invited into God's presence as we are. His presence makes us righteous, worthy, and deserving.

The right time to enter into God's presence is any time. Hear God say to you:

Come to me and I will give you rest—all of you who work so hard beneath a heavy yoke. Wear my yoke—for it fits perfectly—and let me teach you; for I am gentle and humble, and you shall find rest for your souls; for I give you only light burdens.[6]

One way I will enjoy God's presence today and redeem my time is

_____

_____

_____

- Decide to spend meaningful time today with one person who needs to be loved, nurtured, and affirmed. When will you do it? How will you do it?

  _____

  _____

  _____

- Tell God all the ways you enjoy his presence.

  _____

  _____

  _____

- On a separate piece of paper, write down all the religious duties and burdens you carry. Tear up the paper. Come empty-handed to God and discover his acceptance and love for you.

Redeem your time in the presence of God.

The Pain of Division

UNITY AND HARMONY INVITE THE PRESENCE OF God; disunity and division usher out God's presence, replacing his presence with our personal agenda, expectations, intolerance, and need to win.

The tribes of Israel spent years in the Promised Land in a state of confusion, disarray, and disunity. As a result, the presence of God was replaced by attacks, slavery, lack, and suffering. Without unity, God cannot visit our gatherings, families, or communities.

Ever have a verbal altercation around a dinner table? Ever blast a child for doing something wrong, telling him how annoying or clumsy he is? Ever fight with your wife? Did you feel closer to God while fighting and yelling?

Of course, such a query seems absurd, but it dramatically illustrates a foundational truth: Personal intimacy with God is impossible when we are in relational conflict with others.

How is my relationship with God affected when I am angry with others?

_____

_____

_____

Throughout Israel's painful history during the period of the judges (just before Saul, David, and Solomon reigned as kings), they suffered from internal conflict and disunity. The tribes had continual spats and even armed conflicts among themselves. The presence of God was hidden from sight while internal strife took center stage.

At times, a man or woman became intimate with God and was chosen as a leader of Israel. The phrase used for entering God's presence was "the Spirit of the Lord came upon [the name of the leader]." Being in God's presence so empowered one individual that he or she was able to unify and lead an entire nation. But when that charismatic leader died, unity dissipated and God's presence was not pursued.

This cycle became a tiring, debilitating process for everyone in Israel. Such a cycle can also hinder your pursuit of God's presence. Become aware of this unproductive spiritual carousel and get off of it when it occurs. Red flags for this type of behavior are:

➤ The pursuit of selfish interests with no thought for corporate direction or for security in the family, community, or nation.

➤ The disintegration of community followed by strife among families, clans, regions, and tribes.

➤ Constant attacks from outside enemies that destroy communities. Distracted by the pain, suffering, and division, God's presence is forgotten.

The cycle can only be broken when the pain of division is overcome by unifying love among those who seek God's presence together.

How does division and disunity—and the consequent strife and pain—keep me from God's presence?

_____

_____

_____

KEYS TO INVITING GOD'S PRESENCE

⚷ Gather and worship with those of a kindred spirit who desire God's presence as you do. Share together how God's presence has touched and filled your life.

⚷ Go to those with whom you fight and quarrel. Repent and ask their forgiveness. Decide to set aside pain and walk in unity.

🔑 Cry out to God. Ask God's Spirit to come over you as he did for the leaders in ancient Israel. Invite God to use you to unify those around you into a loving, sharing community seeking his presence.

———— ❧ ————

God's presence abides among those
who dwell together in unity.[7]

Lost Identity

WITHOUT GOD'S PRESENCE, WE CANNOT KNOW who we are. In today's Western culture, identity is so rooted in what we *do* that we have lost touch with who we *are*. As long as performance determines self-worth, we won't find the time nor have the desire to seek God's presence.

But often a time comes when staring into an empty mirror becomes a reason to ask, "Who am I?" Belonging gives identity. An individual belonging to a family gives identity. A family belonging to a clan gives identity. A clan belonging to a nation gives identity. A nation belonging to God gives lasting identity.

Israel marched into the future not because she was a great geopolitical empire. Quite the opposite. All she had, but all she needed, was an identity as God's people.

Inviting God's presence goes far beyond individual striving for a personal identity. We must reach out beyond ourselves, our inner pain and fears, to step into God's presence.

When the pain of loneliness becomes greater than the fear of relationship, when the pain of existence becomes greater than the fear of living, when the pain of comfort becomes greater than the fear of risk, when the pain of unknowing becomes greater than the fear of knowing—only then will you step out of self and enter into his presence.

The pain I must overcome to step beyond fear is

_____

_____

_____

We may experience the pain of loneliness because we fear the potential hurts of an intimate relationship with the Other. People tell us of how they have been hurt by God. But what if their hurts are simply projections of blame because they cannot bear the personal responsibility for the consequences of their own misguided and faulty decisions?

We may experience the pain of existence because we fear the metamorphosis that resurrection brings. Life births radical change. Life transforms a gray existence into a rainbow of cinematic colors. Life takes a flat, two-dimensional existence and creates a three-dimensional reality. Instead of just me and you, life becomes community enveloped in Presence. To survive in the land of promise, the Israelites were forced from individual existence into communal cooperation under the leadership of King David driven by God's presence. King David wrote:

> *You will show me the path of life;*
> *In Your presence is fullness of joy;*
> *At Your right hand are pleasures forevermore.* [8]

> *For You have made him most blessed forever;*
> *You have made him exceedingly glad with Your presence.*
> *For the king trusts in the LORD,*
> *And through the mercy of the Most High he shall not be moved.* [9]

Existence can be solitary, but life can only be experienced in community—I and thou and I and Thou. So Jesus prayed, "That they all may be one; as thou, Father, art in me and I in thee, that they also may be one in us: that the world may believe that thou hast sent me." [10]

We experience false comfort behind the faceless mask of solitude. No one knows us, so no one can hurt us. No one touches us so no one can strike us. We fear reaching beyond ourselves, since there is risk in relationship—the risk of being rejected, invaded, dominated, intimidated, and manipulated. We have seen such risk in human relationships. But in God's presence something else happens. We discover a belonging that heals hurts and rewards risk with faithfulness, loyalty, and trust.

> *The Spirit of the LORD GOD is upon Me,*
> *Because the LORD has anointed Me*
> *To preach good tidings to the poor;*
> *He has sent Me to heal the brokenhearted,*
> *To proclaim liberty to the captives,*
> *And the opening of the prison to those who are bound.* [11]

The pain of unknowing will fill us as long as we choose existence over life and loneliness over belonging. We risk being known when we invite God's presence. And being known renders us vulnerable, transparent, and open. Yet, in the risk of being known comes the reward of knowing God's presence. Out of being known comes intimacy in his presence:

> O LORD, you have searched me and known me.
> Such knowledge is too wonderful for me;
> It is high, I cannot attain it.
> Search me, O God, and know my heart;
> Try me, and know my anxieties;
> And see if there is any wicked way in me,
> And lead me in the way everlasting."[12]

When I consider being known by God, I am most fearful of

_____

_____

_____

When I consider being known by God, I am most excited by

_____

_____

_____

KEYS TO INVITING GOD'S PRESENCE

- Identify to whom or what you belong. Does your belonging give you life or a reason to exist? Does your belonging take you out of yourself or drive you into selfishness and self-centeredness?

- What do you fear most about being known by God? (Circle all that apply.)

  Being exposed

  Being judged for sin or wickedness revealed

Being hurt

Being rejected

Being _____

⚿ Describe the feelings and understandings you experienced when you have been known in his presence.

_____

_____

_____

⸻ ✺ ⸻

Inviting God's presence invites
belonging and identity.

Tearing Down the Walls of Mere Existence and Pain

The main thing that keeps me too busy to find his presence is

_____

_____

_____

I am making progress in inviting God's presence when

_____

_____

_____

Time-wasters that rob my life of meaning and purpose in his presence are

_____

_____

_____

Broken relationships and disunity that keep me from his presence must

_____

_____

_____

Being known by God, I find myself (circle all that apply):

Fearing   Running   Hiding   Rejoicing

Belonging   Fellowshipping   Sharing

Trusting   Feeling guilty

Other _____

In God's presence, my existence
is transformed into life.

Tearing Down the Walls of Greed and Guilt

Every one, throughout the year,
should regard himself as if he were half
innocent and half guilty; and should
regard the whole of mankind as half
innocent and half guilty.

If then he commits one more sin, he
presses down the scale of guilt against
himself and the whole world and
causes its destruction.

—MOSES MAIMONIDES,
MAIMONIDES MISHNEH TORAH

Introduction

WE ARE SEPARATED FROM GOD'S PRESENCE BY OUR OWN greed and guilt. The greedy always take and never give. The guilty continually drown in the morass of their past shame and failure.

In Israel's history, King Solomon departed from the ways of his father King David. David, a man after God's own heart, continually sought the presence of God even though at times he sinned grievously. Remarkably, David always repented and returned to God. The desire of David's heart was to be restored and rest continually in God's presence.

> *Have mercy upon me, O God,*
> *According to Your lovingkindness;*
> *According to the multitude of Your tender mercies,*
> *Blot out my transgressions.*
> *Wash me thoroughly from my iniquity,*
> *And cleanse me from my sin.*
>
> *Hide Your face from my sins,*
> *And blot out all my iniquities.*
> *Create in me a clean heart, O God,*
> *And renew a steadfast spirit within me.*
> *Do not cast me away from Your presence,*
> *And do not take Your Holy Spirit from me.*[1]

King Solomon initially sought God's presence. In building the temple, he obediently followed God's plan for a house of worship. But then he departed from God's presence and built pagan temples for his idol-worshipping wives. Instead of repenting, Solomon became greedy as well as guilty. He mercilessly taxed his people and became enamored with wealth, power, and sensual pleasure. Solomon "enculturated" Hebrew religion and lost his hunger for God's presence. His materialistic grasping weakened his hold on desperation for God.

The walls that hinder God's presence in your life that will be exposed and torn down this week are:

Materialism. Materialism produces self-centered greed. Materialism gives rises to hoarding. It is impossible to pursue materialism and God's presence simultaneously. The greed that arises from materialism becomes a cancer that permeates the soul and quenches the spirit.

Greed. Greed gives birth to takers, not givers. We harbor more than we need while others go lacking. Believing we have earned blessings, we refuse to become a blessing to others. Therefore, instead of others serving us out of love, they serve us as slaves who want what we have. Our children learn to grasp instead of give, hoard instead of release, harvest without planting, and take from the poor to influence the rich.

Idolatry. Using people and loving stuff creates idolatry. We make idols out of stuff. The stuff of clothes, electronics, houses, money, leisure, and pleasure become gods to us. Ancient man falsely worshipped stars. We make stars of those who accumulate much stuff and acquire high profiles; then we worship the stars and what they have acquired—even though their stardom is fleeting when put into perspective.

Guilt. Guilt renders seekers helpless. Guilty, we are unable to live freely, give generously, and forgive graciously. Helpless in our pursuit of false gods, we become slaves to things that displease the true God. We are unable to make right choices because all of our idols have been created by creatures, not the Creator.

Helplessness. Seeking God's presence takes spiritual and emotional strength, but often we are too tired, hopeless, and powerless to seek God. Drained by daily tasks and strained relationships and our fruitless pursuit of "stuff," we languish before screens and monitors that flash sterile images of false gods that cannot renew or revive our spirits.

This week, you will move beyond the walls of greed and guilt. You will discover that absolution comes not in introspection or self-cleansing but rather that atonement comes from the very One you seek. In God's presence infinite love and limitless forgiveness are found.

But a point of stumbling awaits every seeker. To find absolution, the seeker must come to a place of confession and repentance—admittance and sorrow. Could it be that the addiction to stuff makes greed more appealing than communion with God? Could it be that the weight of guilt becomes more bearable than the exposure of confession? These are questions you will face in the coming days as you seek to move beyond these walls into God's presence.

DAY 1

Materialism: The Wall of Self-Centered Greed

W HEN IS ENOUGH, ENOUGH? MORE THAN ENOUGH? When does abundance turn into gluttony? Can we on our own stop hoarding and start giving?

Greed detours our pursuit of God's presence. Greed makes selfish concerns— concerns that have no regard for God's presence or direction—a priority. Greed actually elevates stuff to the first priority in our search for meaning and demotes God and others to a lower rank. Greed blocks our view of the invisible. We cannot move forward into God's presence because we are stuck in the mire of material things. As a result, we become slaves to the very stuff we seek. Marketers and advertisers know this. They use sensual messages laced with sex and lust to sell to us as we sit addicted to the television screens in our homes and hotel rooms.

We cannot break the bonds of greed without God's help. Continuing to pursue stuff renders us helpless in our pursuit of his presence. We are pushed farther from him and farther toward destruction. This story reveals the truth of what happens when this wall dominates our lives:

> *The ground of a certain rich man yielded plentifully. And he thought within himself, saying, "What shall I do, since I have no room to store my crops?" So he said, "I will do this: I will pull down my barns and build greater, and there I will store all my crops and my goods. And I will say to my soul, 'Soul, you have many goods laid up for many years; take your ease; eat, drink, and be merry.'" But God said to him, "Fool! This night your soul will be required of you; then whose will those things be which you have provided?" So is he who lays up treasure for himself, and is not rich toward God.*[2]

The sin of greed:

- ➤ Impoverishes us; we become poor toward God and the things of God
- ➤ Elevates selfish desires and lust over God
- ➤ Uses people and loves things
- ➤ Motivates us to become jealous of what others possess
- ➤ Empowers what we possess to possess us
- ➤ Steals from our descendants, leaving them no inheritance
- ➤ Lays barren our future and destiny because we do not sow for a harvest
- ➤ Transforms generosity into stinginess
- ➤ Makes takers out of givers

Instead of having a window into God's presence, greed paints silver on the back of the glass, giving you only a mirror. All you can see in the mirror is your selfish desires motivated by an insatiable hunger that is less and less satisfied. Greed destroys relationships, demeans persons, and defiles intimacy. Such greed becomes all-consuming of every other passion or pursuit in life including finding God's presence.

I am most greedy when I

_____

_____

_____

God's piercing Word—which can tear down the wall of greed—is simple and radical. It was spoken to a rich young man whose possessions had become a wall of greed between God and him.

> _Now behold, one came and said to Him, "Good Teacher, what good thing shall I do that I may have eternal life?" So He said to him, "Why do you call Me good? No one is good but One, that is, God. But if you want to enter into life, keep the commandments." He said to Him, "Which ones?" Jesus said, " 'You shall not murder, You shall not commit adultery, You shall not steal, You shall not bear false witness, Honor your father and your mother,' and, 'You shall love your neighbor as yourself.'" The young man said to Him, "All these things I have kept from my youth. What do I still lack?" Jesus said to him, "If you want to be perfect, go, sell what you have and give to the poor, and you will have treasure in heaven; and come, follow Me." But when the young man heard that saying, he went away sorrowful, for he had great possessions._[3]

Those wants that keep me from the pursuit of God are

_____

_____

_____

KEYS TO INVITING GOD'S PRESENCE

⚷ Describe how greed has hurt relationships in your life.

_____

_____

_____

⚷ With what will you replace your greed?

_____

_____

_____

⚷ What needs to happen within your soul to change you from a taker into a giver? Think about it. Pray about it. Act on it.

_____

_____

_____

*Greed transforms our window to God's
presence into a selfish mirror.*

The Idolatry of Stuff

MATERIALISM COUPLED WITH SOCIAL COMPLEXITY renders our pursuit of God aimless. Our days are filled with endless commercials and ads that beckon us to buy happiness and purchase voyeuristic pleasures. We slave at unfulfilling jobs so we can purchase stuff on credit and make unending installment payments so we own that which never satisfies.

Our possessions possess us, and we idolize them. Idolatry takes many subtle forms in culture. An idol doesn't have to be a carving set in a temple and worshipped with vain and repetitious prayers, burning incense, meaningless sacrifices, or ineffective offerings.

Vain and repetitious prayers. The prayers to our materialistic idols are our spoken (or unspoken) internal desires that yearn to possess, accumulate, complicate, and hoard. We pray, "Gimme, gimme, and please gimme now." But God has a stern warning for us: "Don't recite the same prayer over and over as the heathen do, who think prayers are answered only by repeating them again and again. Remember, your Father knows exactly what you need even before you ask him!"[4]

Burning incense. Before going through a car wash the attendants often ask me, "What scent do you want?" Usually I ask for the "new car" spray. There's something intoxicating about stuff that smells new. Likewise, there's an aversion to old, musty, stale smells. New stuff, which we can elevate quickly into new idols, continually beckons us to sell for pennies on the dollar the items we treasured such a short time ago. So we trash last year's model in exchange for the latest electronic upgrade or model remake. We trade in the car, build a new home—usually larger and certainly more expensive—upgrade the computer, find a new cell phone, or move quickly from analog to digital so our toys are the best and the latest.

Meaningless sacrifices. We sacrifice our health and time to work continually so that we can lease—or, rarely, own—the stuff we so hedonistically grasp. We sacrifice the time we could use to build deep and intimate relationships so we can earn the money to pay for the stuff we must also maintain, insure, and care for. Houses must be painted, yards mowed, cars serviced, boats stored, equipment repaired, and electronics updated so we can "enjoy" the possessions that now possess us.

Ineffective offerings. And the offerings we pay to the credit and installment gods of mammon become the demanding and constant petitions made monthly or more often. Held hostage to our credit reports, we faithfully pay our dues to unseen misers who cajole and threaten us should the offering be too little or too late.

How then shall we exist without our materialistic idols? They must become tools to be used instead of gods to be served. Such tools in the hands of "God-chasers," as described by Tommy Tenney, can be used to build, serve, and give to others. We must learn to manage money instead of credit and use time to invest wisely in people instead of simply pursuing stuff. And we must simplify our lives in order to give, instead of existing just to pay.

My materialistic idol is

_____

_____

_____

Inviting God requires us to step back from the demanding cries of materialistic gods and listen to the still, small voice of the true God who comes to set us free from slavery. He says to us, "I have come that you might have life and have it more abundantly."[5] That offer of life means we must stop shooting up with the drugs of ecstatic, temporal pleasures and begin to lay up treasures in heaven where moth and rust cannot corrupt.

The lover of our souls beckons us to simply pursue Presence and forsake the ephemeral:

My beloved spoke, and said to me:
"Rise up, my love, my fair one,
And come away.
For lo, the winter is past,
The rain is over and gone.
The flowers appear on the earth;
The time of singing has come,
And the voice of the turtledove
Is heard in our land.
The fig tree puts forth her green figs,
And the vines with the tender grapes
Give a good smell.
Rise up, my love, my fair one,
And come away![6]

The perfect ax for cutting down every idolatrous altar is God's love, which reveals every idol for what it truly is—impersonal, unloving, inhuman, and unfeeling. As St. John of the Cross said, "A reciprocal love is actually formed between God and the soul, like the marriage union in which the goods of both (the divine essence which each possesses freely by reason of the voluntary surrender between them) are possessed by both."

What must I let go of to respond to God's beckoning of love?

_____

_____

_____

KEYS TO INVITING GOD'S PRESENCE

When is the next day you can spend with God? When is the next day you can spend devoted to those who love you? What will you do?

_____

_____

_____

‎🗝️ What idolatrous symbols of materialism will you cut up, pay off, and/or throw away forever?

_____

_____

_____

‎🗝️ Write a prayer repenting of materialism and seeking God's presence with greater simplicity.

_____

_____

_____

⸺⦻⸺

The simplicity of God's loving presence helps
us smash the idols of materialism.

Loving Stuff and Using Others

We use others when we idolize stuff. Idolatry makes us slaves to things and motivates us to reduce people to objects we manipulate, legislate, and dominate. When we elevate the impersonal above the personal, we use people to get us what we want. However, long after the stuff passes away, people are still around. After the stuff disappears, will we have any relationships that sustain us?

God's presence empowers us to relate to others as persons through sharing, caring, and giving.

I have held the hands of many dying persons and stood watch over them. Never have I heard them confess that they wish they could have spent more time acquiring stuff or working at the office. But often they have wept over broken relationships that remain unreconciled. Their regrets over lost relationships far outweigh any loss of stuff they may have suffered over the years. Simply put, "He who trusts in his riches will fall."[7]

The pursuit of possessions reduces us to automatons who systematically use people for our own acquisitions. In show business, people are reduced to glittering icons who are groomed and dressed for appearance. But do not touch! They are protected by security systems and bodyguards. They eschew relationships, fearing betrayal, hurt, or exposure.

When we use people, we find ourselves bound by the following destructive relational patterns:

Manipulation. We manipulate people to advance and elevate ourselves to higher levels of power, prestige, and prominence. People become steps in our own personal ladders of success. We step on and over them to get to positions we want. We fire or discard people when they are no longer useful to us.

The antidote to manipulation is partnering. When we win, they win. Their success becomes our success. Together we stand; should we fall, we pick up one another.

> *For if they fall, one will lift up his companion.*
> *But woe to him who is alone when he falls,*
> *For he has no one to help him up.*[8]

Intimidation. Relationships built on fear soon self-destruct. Fear makes us hide, lie, and conceal our innermost faults and failures lest their exposure bring rejection. In God's presence, just the opposite happens. Exposure—confession—brings forgiveness. So the antidote to intimidation must be open confession and ready forgiveness. Over three hundred times in Scripture God's voice, in a plethora of sounds and styles, says, "Fear not."

Legislation. Relationship is built on covenant, not contract. Every contractual relationship is:

➤ Conditional

➤ Temporal

➤ Protection against failure

➤ Insurance for uncertainties

➤ Preparation for defense

➤ Able to be broken

As airtight as humans try to construct the rules, contracts always seem to have loopholes or exit clauses that allow for pain, brokenness, and divorce. Relationships built on rules breed rebellion.

What contractual excuses do I most incorporate or experience in my relationships?

_____

_____

_____

To the contrary, covenant relationships are:

➤ Unconditional

➤ Lasting

➤ Success-oriented

➤ Secure

➤ Open

➤ Unbreakable

God's presence offers covenant for those who are willing to come together and enter into his presence in loving unity. Trying to legislate how we relate to others will ultimately drive them away and remove us from the pursuit of God's presence.

Domination. Using people reduces us to attempting to control another person's thoughts, will, and emotions. Instead of parenting children and developing interdependence, we try to control while fostering dependence. Instead of loving our spouses, we dominate them, using and abusing them emotionally and sexually. Instead of freely worshipping God, religious cults so indoctrinate their adherents that fundamental fanaticism clouds their minds and drives their behaviors to suicidal or murderous violence.

Speaking the truth in love always leaves the other person free to decide, to love, and to respond in their own ways. Freedom always runs the risk of hurt and pain but also always leaves the door open to intimacy and in-depth sharing. So the antidote to domination is freedom to choose and openness to risk.

Why is it that healthy relationships are so important to inviting God's presence? Look at his promise: "When two or more are gathering in my name, there I am in the midst of them."[9] We read of how the early community of God's presence was only visited by his Spirit when they were in "one accord."[10] We hear the divine whisper say, "When you have served the least of these, you have served me."[11] The bridges to God's presence are holistic, healthy relationships. He intimately assures us, "No longer do I call you my disciples . . . but rather my friends."[12]

Relationships I have had that I would like to restore with unconditional love and trust are

_____

_____

_____

KEYS TO INVITING GOD'S PRESENCE

⚷ Name those you have manipulated and describe how you will work toward restoring the relationships.

_____

_____

_____

⚷ Name those you have dominated and describe how you will work toward restoring the relationships.

_____

_____

_____

⚷ Name those you have legislated and describe how you will work toward restoring the relationships.

_____

_____

_____

⚷ Name those you have intimidated and describe how you will work toward restoring the relationships.

_____

_____

_____

Write a prayer asking for God's presence to enter into the restoration of each relationship.

_____

_____

_____

Restored relationships make way for inviting
God's presence into our midst.

Guilt Renders Seekers Helpless

APART FROM GOD'S PRESENCE, MY GUILT CAN BE ignored, tolerated, and overlooked. The closer I come to his presence, however, the more acute my sense of guilt. Only light reveals darkness. Only goodness spotlights evil. Only Presence brings awareness of the ugly nature of guilt.

The place of judgment and examination begins within each of us. We are accountable for our own thoughts and actions. The time of projecting blame on another must be relegated to the past. Excuses only solidify the already existing wall of guilt between ourselves and God's presence.

Those persons with whom I share confidentially and to whom I hold myself accountable are

_____

_____

_____

Adam's lame excuses for disobedience to God only resulted in him and Eve hiding from God's presence. David was comfortable with murder and adultery only until Nathan the prophet pointed out his guilt.

And Nathan did not compare David's actions to any other person's actions. Sure, horizontal comparison always find peers worse than one's self. Seeing the speck of dust in the lives of others, we can always ignore the beam in our own eyes. Yet give consideration to these words of Jesus:

Judge not, that you be not judged. For with what judgment you judge, you will be judged; and with the measure you use, it will be measured back to you. And why *do you look at the speck in your brother's eye, but do not consider the plank in your own eye? Or how can you say to your brother, 'Let me remove the speck from your eye'; and look, a plank is in your own eye? Hypocrite! First remove the plank from your own eye, and then you will see clearly to remove the speck out of your brother's eye. Do not give what is holy to the dogs; nor cast your pearls before swine, lest they trample them under their feet, and turn and tear you in pieces.*[13]

You will admit your guilt when you:

➢ Are tired of hiding from his presence

➢ Stop comparing the lesser evil in you to the greater evil in others

➢ Begin to come out of the dark into the light

➢ Admit blindness to your own sin and the need to receive sight from One who sees you as you really are

➢ Accept the reality of absolute truth

The statement above that most fits me right now is

_____

_____

_____

Without absolute truth there is no guilt. In God's presence abides absolute truth—that which is true for all people at all times and in all places. Relativism dilutes truth to what's true some of the time for some people in some places.

Relativism advocates that some people are guilty of certain things under certain circumstances. Absolute truth holds all people accountable to the same truth all of the time in every situation. Absolute truth never abides in another person. "No one is good, but One, that is God."[14]

Without comparing our actions and thoughts to the character of God, we cannot discern what is good and true; likewise, we cannot admit or confess what is corrupt or evil.

Only God can tell the saintly from the suburban,
Counterfeit values always resemble the true.[15]

Pursuing God's presence will increasingly expose every private thought and hidden action to the light: "All that is now hidden will someday come to light."[16]

If you desire his presence, prepare yourself for exposure. Presence always brings to light whatever has been thought or done in darkness. That is why people prefer lifeless ritual to true worship. No ritual ever pierced beneath the surface to uncover the true motives of a participant. No idol ever revealed the thoughts and intentions of the heart.

Penitents, not observers, enter into God's presence. And penance requires confession followed by repentance—turning away from darkness to light, from sin to righteousness, from oppression to justice. Every saint first admitted to being a sinner. They understood that "all have sinned and fall short of the glory of God."[17]

The wall of guilt renders us helpless to enter into God's presence. But there is a key to the door that opens into Presence. That key is confession and repentance. "That's harsh," you may protest. Refusing to debate with your protests or field your excuses, God simply replies:

"Come now, and let us reason together,"
Says the LORD,
"Though your sins are like scarlet,
They shall be as white as snow;
Though they are red like crimson,
They shall be as wool.

"If you are willing and obedient,
You shall eat the good of the land;
But if you refuse and rebel,
You shall be devoured by the sword."[18]

Tearing down the wall of guilt requires that you:

➤ Admit or confess your sin

➤ Receive forgiveness, mercy, and cleansing from God

➤ Admit that you are helpless to forgive or cleanse yourself

➤ Receive God's strength to walk in the light and obey his voice

➤ Admit that in his presence is all truth

➤ Receive his power to know the truth and be set free from guilt and sin

The face of God comes to you saying simply, "I am the way, the truth, and the life. No one comes to the Father except through Me."[19]

Closing my eyes, I see the loving face of God communicating to me that

_____

_____

_____

KEYS TO INVITING GOD'S PRESENCE

🔑 Describe any guilt or sin in your life that blocks God's presence and hinders your pursuit of him.

_____

_____

_____

🔑 Write a simple prayer asking God to forgive you. Or go back to this week's introduction and pray out loud the prayer of King David beginning, "Have mercy on me, O God."

_____

_____

_____

🔑 Receiving and accepting forgiveness is often difficult. Circle those things that make it hard for you to receive forgiveness.

Self-condemnation

The condemnation of others

The inability to let go of the past

Other _____

—⊗⊗⊗—

Confession, repentance, and accepting forgiveness
open a door into God's presence.

DAY 5

The Wall of Separation

CONDEMNING OURSELVES AND JUDGING OTHERS BUILD walls—of addictive sin or of self-righteousness. Being condemned by others and accepting their condemnation can distance us from others and from God's presence.

Separation arising out of self-condemnation. Condemning ourselves is the result of believing the lie that we can never be forgiven. Destructive and deceitful thoughts fill our minds:

> ➤ I fail therefore I am a failure.

> ➤ My sin is too great for anyone to forgive.

> ➤ Because I don't feel forgiven, I cannot be forgiven.

> ➤ Until I forgive myself, I cannot be forgiven.

> ➤ I am helplessly addicted to sin.

> ➤ Given the past I've had, I can never change.

> ➤ I've tried to change, but I can't. Therefore, I will always be helpless and hopeless.

I must stop condemning myself for

_____

_____

_____

These lies may have been perpetuated by the demonic tongues of those around you or the attacking spirits within you. Regardless of their source, they have no power over the forgiving love of God. The loving presence of God within you is greater than any condemning force in the world.[20] When we accept God's forgiveness, his love overcomes self-condemnation: "In whatever our heart condemns us; for God is greater than our heart and knows all things. Beloved, if our heart does not condemn us, we have confidence before God."[21]

Separation arising from condemnation from others. Others will persecute and even condemn you. They may be accurate in their condemnations, but their attitude will be one of self-righteousness. They have failed to live by the creed "Judge not that you be not judged."[22] Often they judge the very sin in others that is most prevalent in their own lives.

You cannot allow their self-righteousness to deter you from the pursuit of God. The narrative is told of an adulterous woman who was about to be stoned to death by the self-righteous religious teachers in her community. A loving teacher entered the situation and was asked if the law condemning her to death should be followed. His classic reply is also spoken to you: "He who is without sin among you, let him throw a stone at her first."[23]

Refuse to allow the self-righteous judgment of others who seek to condemn you and thereby derail your pursuit of God's presence. Ask God's Spirit to reveal to you whatever sin is in you. "And when he [God's Spirit] has come he will convince the world of its sin, and of the availability of God's goodness, and of deliverance from judgment."[24] Listen to God's voice speaking through your conscience. His voice will speak truth in love for correction of your thoughts and actions.

Discard self-condemnation and the condemnation of others. Listen to the only voice that counts—the loving voice of God's presence. No form of condemnation can separate you from the love of God.

I refuse to be separated from the love of God because

_____

_____

_____

⚷ When others condemn or your inner self attacks, meditate on these thoughts. Inhale and say the first truth. Exhale and say the second truth.

> *[inhale]* God loves me
> *[exhale]* And doesn't condemn me

> *[inhale]* I love me
> *[exhale]* Because God loves me

> *[inhale]* No one has the right to judge me
> *[exhale]* For God is my judge

> *[inhale]* I will only listen
> *[exhale]* To words of life and blessing spoken over me

⚷ List all the ways God has shown you that he loves you.

_____

_____

_____

⚷ Write down every self-condemning thought you have on a piece of paper and burn it. As it burns, affirm this truth: "God loves me with an everlasting love."

───⊷⊷⊷───

*God's presence shatters the condemnation
of others and of self.*

Tearing Down the Walls of Greed and Guilt

I am tearing down the wall of greed by

_____

_____

_____

One way I need to eliminate the idolatry of stuff in my life is

_____

_____

_____

I know that God doesn't condemn me because

_____

_____

_____

In God's presence, forgiveness is

_____

_____

_____

Ways I need to show love to others this week are

_____

_____

_____

Tearing Down the Walls of Unworthiness and Legalism

This young woman [in the concentration camp] knew that she would die in the next few days. But when I talked to her she was cheerful in spite of this knowledge. "I am grateful that fate has hit me so hard," she told me.

"In my former life I was spoiled and did not take spiritual accomplishments seriously." Pointing through the window of the hut, she said, "This tree here is the only friend I have in my loneliness." Through that window she could see just one branch of a chestnut tree, and on the branch were two blossoms.

"I often talk to this tree," she said to me. I was startled and didn't quite know how to take her words. Was she delirious? Did she have occasional hallucinations? Anxiously I asked her if the tree replied.

"Yes." What did it say to her? She answered, "It said to me, 'I am here—I am life, eternal life.'"

—VIKTOR FRANKL,
MAN'S SEARCH FOR MEANING

Introduction

HAVE YOU EVER FELT LIKE YOU SHOULD BE ABLE TO EARN your way in whatever area of life you find yourself? As an employee you want to earn your salary. As a spouse you want to earn the trust and respect of your mate. As a parent you want to earn a place of honor in the eyes of your children. As a child you want to earn a position of pride and esteem from your parents.

The desire to earn our way lies deeply imbedded in our psyche. It arises from the need to feel worthy and significant. Our search for significance leads us on journeys through the corridors of universities and schools, conferences and seminars, books and training courses. But should our search for significance get bogged down or sidetracked—and it always seems to hit various snags—then we begin to doubt ourselves, our abilities, strengths, giftings, and perseverance.

This search for significance in modern society closely resembles what Viktor Frankl called man's search for meaning. Even in the most dire of circumstances, in the Nazi prison camps for Jews during the holocaust of World War II, Frankl observed humans treated like animals desperately striving to find meaning in the midst of hopeless tragedy and persecution.

> The odds of surviving the camp were no more than one in twenty-eight . . . It did not seem possible, let alone probable, that the manuscript of my first book, which I had hidden in my coat when I arrived at Auschwitz, would ever be rescued . . . So I found myself confronted with the question whether under such circumstances my life was ultimately void of any meaning.
>
> Not yet did I notice that an answer to this question with which I was wrestling so passionately was already in store for me, and that soon thereafter this answer would be given to me. This was the case when I had to surrender my clothes and in turn inherited the worn-out rags of an inmate who had already been sent to the

gas chamber immediately after his arrival at the Auschwitz railway station. Instead of the many pages of my manuscript, I found in a pocket of the newly acquired coat one single page torn out of a Hebrew prayer book, containing the most important Jewish prayer, Shema Yisrael.[1]

The Shema Yisrael reads, "Hear, O Israel: The LORD our God, the LORD is one! You shall love the LORD your God with all your heart, with all your soul, and with all your strength."[2] God has some unusual ways of making his presence known to us even in the most desperate circumstances of life!

Even when we don't hit the bumps of self-doubt along the road to meaning in our lives, others are quick to point out their doubts about us. Critical, judgmental, or jealous, our detractors, who often masquerade as our friends, point out every flaw so we will certainly know how frail and accident-prone our efforts are. At some juncture along life's road, we come to the dead-end street called *unworthiness*. Too often we camp there and, at times, become permanent roadside residents of the ditch labeled, "I am not, I cannot be, and I never will be a person of worth."

We construct this wall of unworthiness from the bricks of self-pity and abuse, which are held together with the mortar of victimization. Believing ourselves victims of our own failures, we never see ourselves worthy of receiving any good thing from anyone else. Most of all, we see ourselves unworthy of being loved by a perfect God whose holiness and purity immediately expose our every flaw and weakness. We imagine that we appear so base in his sight that he would never bother with, as the great hymn "Amazing Grace" says, "such a wretch as I."

Overcoming insignificance. Our feelings of unworthiness lead us to believe that we can never earn the love, respect, or esteem of another. Feeling overwhelmed by the insignificance of our place in the human existence, we think we are only a speck of dust among billions of people on a tiny, obscure planet lost in a vast universe. So even if we pursued and by chance stumbled upon God's presence, he would not even recognize or appreciate our efforts. Like an annoying fly, we would be swatted away by a cosmic hand that had no concern for such insignificant, worthless, meaningless irritants like us.

Receiving worth. If worth and significance cannot be earned, how then can they be received? We learn from early childhood there's no such thing as a free lunch. If we can't earn worth, we must be doomed to live in unworthiness. Surprisingly, we will discover that God's presence cannot be earned and that even before developing an intimate relationship with God we are accepted and deemed important and worthy. Such unmerited grace gives us pause and makes us wonder: Is this too good to be true?

Religious legalism. One of the greatest contributors to our feelings of unworthiness is our invariable inability to keep the rules and obey the laws instituted by religious authorities. We discover that perhaps the greatest obstacles to our pursuit of God's presence are the ladders to nowhere that religion dictates we climb. Religion tells us what we must do in order to earn God's love and acceptance. Yet the very things we are told we must do we often cannot bring ourselves to accomplish.

> *For I know that in me (that is, in my flesh) nothing good dwells; for to will is present with me, but how to perform what is good I do not find. For the good that I will to do, I do not do; but the evil I will not to do, that I practice. Now if I do what I will not to do, it is no longer I who do it, but sin that dwells in me. I find then a law, that evil is present with me, the one who wills to do good.*[3]

It's not a lack of desire on our parts, for we desperately hunger for God's presence. Rather, we find ourselves without strength. Simply put, we are weak and helpless to become the good people the religious authorities demand we become. Always falling short of keeping the law, religion keeps us bound to our weaknesses.

Beyond religion to relationship. Inviting God's presence takes us beyond the dictates of the religious self-righteous and into the uncharted waters of mercy and grace. If significance and worth are indeed gifts given and imparted to those who seek them, then how can they be received? Through relationship. Religion is governed by rules and law, but relationship is rooted in love. Expecting to find religion at the center of God's presence we, like C. S. Lewis, will be surprised by joy to find someone, not something, waiting for us.

In this final week of tearing down the walls that impede your pursuit of God's presence, you will discover that waiting for you on the other side of your walls is God, who has been there waiting all the time.

Overcoming Insignificance

"I'M NOT WORTHY TO RECEIVE GOD'S LOVE AND MERCY," moaned a hopeless penitent. Many of us feel as though we cannot be accepted unless we purify ourselves first and make ourselves acceptable. Living in such a vast universe among billions of people, we wonder if a pure and infinite God could love us and enter into relationship with us when we are so unworthy.

Entering his presence does not depend on *our* worthiness. Rather, entering in depends on *his* grace and mercy. We enter God's presence not because we have earned the right to be near him but only because his nature is merciful and gracious.

> *God is so rich in mercy. He loved us so much that even though we were spiritually dead and doomed by our sins he gave us back our lives again when he raised Christ from the dead—for only by his undeserved favor have we ever been saved—and lifted us up from the grave into glory along with Christ. We sit with him in the heavenly realms all because of what Christ did. And now God can always point to us as examples of how very, very rich his kindness is, as shown in all he has done for us through Jesus Christ.*
>
> *Because of his kindness, you have been saved through trusting Christ. And even trusting is not of yourselves; it too is a gift from God. Salvation is not a reward for the good we have done, so none of us can take any credit for it.*[4]

Notice that we sit with him in heavenly places. That is, we are in his presence because of his rich mercy and love. Religion tempts us with the trap of earning love. But earned love isn't *agape*—unconditional acceptance. Love is a gift, or it isn't love. Love imparts worth; it doesn't require worth.

Growing up, I had a stuffed animal, a puppy dog, that I loved so much that most of the fur and even the eyes had been rubbed off from constant playing and sleeping with it. Over the years, my mother tried to get me to give up this favorite toy and adopt a new one. But I never wanted to give it up. I loved it. It was worthless to everyone else in the world but me. My love for it made that puppy priceless.

Intrinsically, we may be filled with guilt, shame, failure, and mistakes, but God's love for us imparts infinite worth to us. Love imparts significance. That ragged stuffed puppy had no intrinsic value, but my love made it of worth to me. So it is with God's love. From conception, his presence has surrounded us.

> *For thou didst form my inward parts,*
>   *thou didst knit me together in my mother's womb.*
> *I praise thee, for thou art fearful and wonderful.*
> *Wonderful are thy works!*
> *Thou knowest me right well;*
>   *my frame was not hidden from thee,*
>   *when I was being made in secret,*
>   *intricately wrought in the depths of the earth.*
> *Thy eyes beheld my unformed substance;*
>   *in thy book were written, every one of them,*
>   *the days that were formed for me,*
>   *when as yet there was none of them.*[5]

The phrase in this Scripture that most touches me is

_____

_____

_____

For a moment, consider the feelings inspired deep within when you're in the presence of a very important dignitary. Standing near a president, king, prime minister, or person of high rank, one feels significant, important, and worthwhile, and the encounter becomes pregnant with meaning. So much so that for years afterward the moment is cherished as one of the most meaningful encounters of a lifetime.

Now consider that from the womb, you have been "standing in the presence" of the universe's creator, by and through whom all things are held together. The fact that others have also been in his presence does not diminish the significance of such an encounter. Rather, it simply points to the reality that each and every person possesses infinite worth, not because it was earned, but rather because he or she has been in the presence of the only One who can ultimately impart true significance.

To this end, Paul of Tarsus proclaimed this message from Mars Hill in Athens:

And [God] has made from one blood every nation of men to dwell on all the face of the earth, and has determined their preappointed times and the boundaries of their dwellings, so that they should seek the Lord, in the hope that they might grope for Him and find Him, though He is not far from each one of us; for in Him we live and move and have our being, as also some of your own poets have said, "For we are also His offspring."[6]

Insignificance is overcome when we receive the gift of God's love. It is the singular reality that imparts meaning to our lives.

What keeps me from receiving the gift of God's presence?

_____

_____

_____

KEYS TO INVITING GOD'S PRESENCE

Remember the times when you felt most insignificant. What made you feel that way?

_____

_____

_____

When did you realize that God deems you significant?

_____

_____

_____

- ☞ Meditate on the wonder of your intricate creation. Set aside the theories of how you were created and allow yourself simply to stand in awe and wonder that you exist as you do—that you are no accident in the universe!

- ☞ Write a prayer of thanksgiving for the reality that even in the womb God's presence surrounded you, imparting both meaning and significance.

_____

_____

_____

—⚬⚬⚬—

The creative presence of God imparted significance
to you from conception.

DAY 2

Receiving Worth

Rushing through the floral district of China Town in Kuala Lumpur one day, I refused to receive all the fragrances, beauty, and visual still-life portraits that hung briefly on the easel of my senses. Had I paused to enjoy the experience, those moments would have overflowed with meaning and worth. But my schedule was more important, and that time is now but a blur in my memory.

Another time, backpacking through the Rockies, my group and I happened upon a meadow blanketed with wildflowers. I vividly remember Horse Thief Meadow. I can still see the rainbow of colors and smell the myriad perfumes of nature, because we paused to drink in the meaning of the moment.

Demolish the wall of rushing. To receive worth, we must demolish the wall of rushing and begin to enjoy the journey. In celebration, traveling down M. Scott Peck's *The Road Less Traveled,* we must find a way to exit the world's superhighways and ramble along the country roads that wind their way through the landscapes of life.

Yes, taking time to receive worth may inconvenience us in the pursuit of pleasure or stuff. But taking time to find God's presence and invite his presence into our lives means each moment is filled with ultimate worth.

How often we find ourselves moaning, "Well, that certainly wasn't worth my time!" If it wasn't worth our time, then why did we give ourselves to it? Perhaps we have boarded the train, rushed through life, and forgotten to get off at the right stop. I remember riding the Philadelphia subway and becoming so engrossed in a book that I missed my stop and went miles out of my way, losing hours in my day. I had become so preoccupied in a task that I missed out on where I was going.

Mundane tasks can so occupy our attention that we never look up to see where we are going or how we are getting there. Consequently, by the time we get to the end of the route, we have rushed by all the meaningful stops in life and have failed to receive the many worthwhile relationships and encounters they offered.

My self-worth is rooted in

_____

_____

_____

God's presence imparts worth. But in the flurry of our existence, we may fail to receive what God wishes to give. We rush out the back door of life while God stands at the front door with a special delivery of meaning and worth for us. We never hear the doorbell ringing. We never sign for the delivery. Why? We are in such a hurry to jump into the car, get on the cell phone, and speed to our next meeting that we miss the most important meeting of all—finding God's presence.

Take the time and effort to receive. It takes time to receive worth—to listen and to pray, to ponder and to meditate, to study and to read both Word and words. If a friend mails me a large check, the fact that the check is in the mail doesn't mean I have received the worth. I must go to the mailbox. I must open the letter. I must endorse the check, take it to the bank, and deposit it. Only after time and effort do I grasp the worth of it.

Inviting God's presence requires more than seeking; it demands receiving. The first-century proclamation rings true today: "Repent, be baptized and receive the gift of the Holy Spirit."[7] In the journey to find God's presence, we must come to the point of making the decision to receive worth from God or to reject it. As a gift, his presence is freely given, but just like any gift, presence doesn't enter uninvited.

He was in the world, and the world was made through Him, and the world did not know Him. He came to His own, and His own did not receive Him. But as many as received Him, to them He gave the right to become children of God, to those who believe in His name: who were born, not of blood, nor of the will of the flesh, nor of the will of man, but of God.[8]

God never forces himself on us. Simply acknowledging his existence does not constitute finding his presence. What's truly worthwhile lies in receiving his presence.

How willing am I to receive what's truly worthwhile—his presence?

_____

_____

_____

KEYS TO INVITING GOD'S PRESENCE

⚿ List the times in your schedule for today that you have set aside for receiving God's presence.

_____

_____

_____

⚿ What must you stop doing that is worthless so that you can receive worth from God?

_____

_____

_____

⚿ Write a description of God's perspective of your worth and value.

_____

_____

_____

*Upon finding God's presence, I must receive
the worth he imparts to me.*

The Wall of Religious Legalism

LEGALISM FINDS BOTH WAYS AND REASONS TO DENY us entry into God's presence. Legalism locks and bolts shut the doors into his presence. Legalism points out why we are never worthy to enter into his presence. Legalism reduces relationship to a set of rules that, when any one of them is broken, causes the relationship to be lost.

Can any set of rules or laws define a relationship? Jesus of Nazareth taught we need a relationship with God the Father. The religious rulers around him kept pointing out all the ways he was breaking their rules. Yet the religious laws and traditions had become fences that kept people out of God's presence. Sinners couldn't enter into his presence because they were lost. The righteous couldn't enter into his presence because they were so focused on the rules that they completely bypassed a relationship with God.

Rules designate what we can and can't do, but they cannot form or replace a relationship. Relationships are not organized rules and duties that one fulfills. A marriage relationship doesn't constantly check a contract to see if all is well. A relationship in marriage says, "Nothing you can do will make me stop loving you." A marriage based on rules will never last.

Rules and contracts are filled with conditions. While rules can help set boundaries they can never anticipate every contingency. They are limited in being able to describe relationships and they can never force relationships.

Certainly God's presence has boundaries for holiness, purity, and righteousness. But his boundaries protect us, and when a breakout occurs, repentance and forgiveness are the means to restoration.

A woman is caught in adultery. She has broken the rules and deserves to die. The legalists and self-righteous judges stand around her, ready to stone her to death. When they bring the woman to Jesus, he, surprisingly, speaks more harshly and bluntly to the judges than to the sinner. Writing in the sand, he exposes their legalism as well as their hypocrisy. "Let him without sin cast the first stone." All the religious legalists left the scene. Only the woman and Jesus remained. Only the relationship was left after the rules had failed to bring justice and mercy into the situation.

Laws can only define; they can never constitute a relationship. Rules always get broken, but a relationship can overcome and persevere even when the traditions are transgressed. Jesus observed that people make the word of God "of no effect by applying the traditions of men."[9] At times relationship transcends being right. Law killed the Christ, but love raised him from the dead. Law could not conquer love; rules could not end relationship.

Religious legalism may be keeping you from a relationship with God. You may feel you must become righteous before you can find God's presence. But God's presence is offered not *because of* what you do but *in spite of* what you do. What you do can't make things right with God. But God can come into your life through mercy and grace to meet every condition of the law. What the law cannot do, relationship can.

All around you people may be offering suggestions on what to do and how to do it. Relax. Be still. Know God. The law and religious legalism can make you aware of the lack of God's presence in your life, but they can never usher you into God's presence.

When I am still, I feel (Mark an X to indicate your feelings):

Anxious — Hopeful

Calm — Agitated

Productive — Wasteful

Before Christ, according to the law something always had to die in order for one to enter into God's presence. So animals were sacrificed. Food and grain were sacrificed. Still, only a select few entered into God's presence on just one day a year called atonement. But then God provided a way to enter into his presence through mercy that satisfied his justice.

"No man could see God and live" was the way of the law. But God's presence seeks relationship, not rules. Only he was able to fulfill the rules so we could enter into his presence, and that's precisely what he did.

> *Now, when sins have once been forever forgiven and forgotten, there is no need to offer more sacrifices to get rid of them.*
>
> *And so, dear brothers, now we may walk right into the very Holy of Holies, where God is, because of the blood of Jesus. This is the fresh, new, life-giving way that Christ has opened up for us by tearing the curtain—his human body—to let us into the holy presence of God.*[10]

There's a price to be paid when someone breaks the religious rules. But if God provided a way for the price to be paid through Christ, what is our part in entering into God's presence?

To receive.

Once we have torn down the walls and found that presence has a face, we recognize that face-to-face relationships cost something. A face-to-face relationship with Christ confronts us with the stark reality of his words, "Greater love has no one than this, that he lay down his life for his friends."[11] What a tremendous price he was willing to pay in order to call us "friend." Friendship goes far beyond the demands of legalism in order to demonstrate unconditional love.

> *God showed his great love for us by sending Christ to die for us while we were still sinners. And since by his blood he did all this for us as sinners, how much more will he do for us now that he has declared us not guilty? Now he will save us from all the wrath to come. And since, when we were his enemies, we were brought back to God by the death of his son, what blessings he must have for us now that we are his friends and he is living within us!*
>
> *Now we rejoice in our wonderful new relationship with God—all because of what our Lord Jesus Christ has done in dying for our sins—making us friends of God.*[12]

Presence brings us into relationship with God as friends, not as enemies; we become relational, not religious. Remember, *presence* in the Hebrew literally means "before the face." When we tear down wall after wall and earnestly seek his face, we turn the corner only to find God was always there—waiting patiently.

To our surprise, Christ calmly says, "He who has seen me has seen the Father."[13] God's presence has a face.

Religious legalism fails to

_____

_____

_____

KEYS TO INVITING GOD'S PRESENCE

⚯ How do you feel when faced with a multitude of religious rules? (Circle all that apply.)

Condemned	Guilty	Overwhelmed
Defeated	Controlled	Manipulated
Intimidated	Frustrated	Angry

⚯ List the qualities of a best friend.

_____

_____

_____

⚯ How is God like a best friend?

_____

_____

God's presence shatters legalism
through relationship.

Beyond Religion to Relationship

RELIGION PROJECTS PRESENCE AS BEYOND OUR reach and impossible to attain. Religion guards God's presence with ritual and mysticism. Only the esoteric can approach and only the priest can enter when presence is prescribed by religion.

But through relationship, God's presence transforms each seeker into a priest and each person into a tabernacle of his presence. "Don't you realize that all of you together are the house of God, and that the Spirit of God lives among you in his house? If anyone defiles and spoils God's home, God will destroy him. For God's home is holy and clean, and you are that home."[14]

It's time to move beyond religion to relationship through Christ by entering into God's presence. Consider the differences:

➤ Religion focuses on rules. Relationship fixes on presence.

➤ Religion closes the door to the holy of holies. Relationship opens the door.

➤ Religion demands sacrifice. Relationship willingly offers sacrifice.

➤ Religion excludes. Relationship includes.

➤ Religion uplifts the external. Relationship bonds with the internal.

➤ Religion constructs the visible and carves out the idolatrous. Relationship connects with the invisible and crushes the idolatrous.

➤ Religion concerns itself with style. Relationship hungers for substance.

➤ Religion promotes performance. Relationship thirsts for presence.

- ➤ Religion sets boundaries and maintains distance. Relationship invites intimacy.
- ➤ Religion makes buildings into churches. Relationship transforms people into churches.

Inviting God's presence has nothing to do with religion and everything to do with relationship.

I am trapped in religion when I

_____

_____

_____

The central concept that shatters legalism and replaces it with intimacy is covenant. Covenant is a lasting relationship that bonds God's presence with your personhood based on love, not rules. In fact, love becomes the law of covenant relationship.

Pay all your debts except the debt of love for others—never finish paying that! For if you love them, you will be obeying all of God's laws, fulfilling all his requirements.

If you love your neighbor as much as you love yourself you will not want to harm or cheat him, or kill him or steal from him. And you won't sin with his wife or want what is his, or do anything else the Ten Commandments say is wrong. All ten are wrapped up in this one, to love your neighbor as you love yourself.

Love does no wrong to anyone. That's why it fully satisfies all of God's requirements. It is the only law you need.[15]

God's presence enfolds us in his arms of love.

What religious chains do I need to shed to enter into God's presence?

_____

_____

_____

🗝 Describe how religion has distanced you from God's presence.

_____

_____

_____

🗝 As a house of his presence, worship, sing, pray, read Scripture, and invite others seeking God's presence to join you.

🗝 Complete the following:

I have experienced God's presence outside of religion when

_____

_____

_____

Experience God's presence
through relationship.

DAY 5

Coming to the End of Self

THE RESULT OF SELF-TRIUMPHING IN THE GARDEN OF Eden was the loss of God's presence. We read how Adam and Eve hid from God's presence in order to preserve their lonely idolatry of self.

Inviting God's presence brings us to the end of self. We die to selfish interests in order to enter into a relationship with the Other. We begin to look outside ourselves in our pursuit of his presence.

But that pursuit encounters wall after wall that we have built to keep us isolated in our worldly temples of self-centered egoism. We each must make a choice between selfish pursuits and godly pursuit. We cannot move in opposite directions.

Ancient Abram sought God's presence, out from the environs of Ur and into a wandering pursuit of faith and friendship embodied in passionate seeking. Across the generations of seeking, Abram—later called Abraham, meaning "father of nations" and "the friend of God"—fathered a nation of seekers through Isaac, Jacob, and Joseph.

Out of the desperation of slavery, Israel followed the cloud of God's presence into a wilderness wandering that took her from a mountain covered with his presence to a promised land filled with the opportunity to abundantly enjoy his presence. Yet, this vagabond confederacy of tribes lacked the cohesion to pursue God's presence without incorporating the counterfeits of Presence offered by their neighbors in Canaan.

Then King David arrived. He sought God's face and desired to build God's house, which was finally completed during the reign of King Solomon. At that moment the presence of God so flooded his people that Eden's intimacy with God was briefly tasted. At the dedication of the temple, Solomon prayed:

Now therefore,
*Arise, O L*ord *God, to Your resting place,*
You and the ark of Your strength.
*Let Your priests, O L*ord *God, be clothed with salvation,*
And let Your saints rejoice in goodness.
*O L*ord *God, do not turn away the face of Your Anointed;*
Remember the mercies of Your servant David.

When Solomon had finished praying, fire came down from heaven and consumed the burnt offering and the sacrifices; and the glory of the Lord filled the temple. And the priests could not enter the house of the Lord, because the glory of the Lord had filled the Lord's house. When all the children of Israel saw how the fire came down, and the glory of the Lord on the temple, they bowed their faces to the ground on the pavement, and worshipped and praised the Lord, saying:

"For He is good,
For His mercy endures forever."[16]

But God's presence did not permanently abide in a temple built with hands. And the people soon forgot the goodness and mercy of his presence and once again sought the idols and gods of foreign lands. After generations of seeking and then building walls to block out God's presence, the people finally desperately cried out for one anointed with Presence just as Adam and Eve had been in the garden.

When I worship, how do I cry out for God's presence?

_____

_____

_____

This person would be the second Adam. This would be one who so abided in God that those who befriended him would also be God's friends. This one would be God's presence with a face. Such Presence would be intimate and personal. Such Presence would be loving and forgiving. Such Presence could bring one face-to-face with God. Such Presence would be lasting, not temporal.

"But this precious treasure—this light and power that now shine within us—is held in a perishable container. That is, in our weak bodies. Everyone can see that the glorious power within must be from God and is not our own."[17]

The relationship with God's presence will now become the focus of our pursuit. Inviting his presence pushes us deeper and deeper into intimacy with God through his Spirit. Once in God's presence, we will find him to be:

➢ Our companion

➢ Our communicator

➢ Our comforter

➢ Our mentor

➢ Our reconciler

➢ Our encourager

➢ Our holiness

➢ The lover of our souls

Invite God's presence and discover intimacy with the eternal.

My relationship with God is

_____

_____

_____

KEYS TO INVITING GOD'S PRESENCE

Describe how your relationship with God has grown in the last few weeks.

_____

_____

_____

With whom can you study, pray, share, and pursue God's presence? List friends of God who share your pursuit.

_____

_____

_____

Play a tape or CD of worship, praise, or instrumental inspirational music. As you listen for God's voice, enjoy his presence.

We must look beyond self to see God's face.

Tearing Down the Walls of Unworthiness and Legalism

I am significant because

_____

_____

_____

I can receive worth from God because

_____

_____

_____

Legalism detracts me from my relationship with God by

_____

_____

_____

Religion affects me by

_____

_____

_____

I relate to God when

_____

_____

_____

The window to God's presence
is the face of Christ.

Listening and Abiding in God's Presence

That practice which is alike the most holy, the most general, and the most needful in the spiritual life is the practice of the Presence of God. It is the schooling of the soul to find its joy in His Divine Companionship, holding with Him at all times and at every moment humble and loving converse, without set rule or stated method, in all time of our temptation and tribulation, in all time of our dryness of soul and disrelish of God, yes, and even when we fall into unfaithfulness and actual sin.

—BROTHER LAWRENCE,
THE SPIRITUAL MAXIMS OF BROTHER LAWRENCE

Introduction

Inviting God's presence requires listening. Intimacy in God's presence involves not only listening, but also obediently abiding with him. Without listening we cannot know God. And knowing God involves a stillness that renders every other voice silent save his.

Abiding begins with listening and hearing what God says. But true listening cannot exist without obedience. Hearing and obeying flow together like hydrogen and oxygen in water. Without both elements, intimate abiding does not happen.

Many find God's presence for a moment. A moment in worship, prayer, study, silence, music, serving, witnessing, or giving can become an invitation for God's presence. Simply to gather together in obedient faith invites God's presence. Jesus said, "I also tell you this—if two of you agree down here on earth concerning anything you ask for, my Father in heaven will do it for you. For where two or three gather together because they are mine, I will be right there among them."[1]

Why is it that when the walls come down and we finally hear his voice, enter his presence, and experience relationship instead of religion, our encounter with God's presence is often brief and transient? Could it be that God is fickle and unconcerned? Certainly not! The promise of presence is easily understood: "Abide in Me, and I in you. As the branch cannot bear fruit of itself, unless it abides in the vine, neither can you, unless you abide in Me. I am the vine, you are the branches. He who abides in Me, and I in him, bears much fruit; for without Me you can do nothing."[2] So the possibility of abiding is real, but the responsibility for abiding rests with us.

This week we will discover the importance of listening in order to find and walk in his presence. From listening, we will move to obeying what we hear in his presence. From obedience, we will discover that his presence empowers us to develop intimacy as well as to accomplish much.

Be silent and listen. God's presence speaks to us from behind a veil of worldly cacophony. The loud noises and distractions of competing voices often drown the still, small voice of God. How do we continue to listen when the volume of other voices seems to obliterate the voice of his presence?

Hear and obey. Once we have heard God's voice, will we be willing to obey or at least be willing to be made willing? His presence seems to melt away like the morning mist when we fail to act upon what we have heard him whisper into our spirit.

Let go and draw near. Letting go of every distraction from the past, including our sin and separation, may not be easy. We have followed so long the pied pipers of this world that we fail to hear the lasting melodies sung from the heart of God.

Abide intimately. Abiding speaks of constancy and closeness. We cannot abide in God's presence if we come in one moment and leave the next. In marriage, intimacy develops. In marriage, unlike all other relationships, there is a constancy and closeness that develops deeper and deeper intimacy.

Bear fruit. Finding God's presence and abiding in him produces fruit. Something of an enduring and eternal nature is birthed from being in his presence. What is that fruit and how can it be continually growing and multiplying in our relationship with God?

We cannot enter his presence without being changed. We may temporarily change in the presence of another person in order to impress, be accepted, or find favor. But we are not changed by another person; we are changed in God's presence.[3] That change produces fruit in our lives that makes us more like him and also creates a hunger and thirst for his presence in the lives of others.

Be Still and Listen

God's presence had virtually disappeared from the people. They had pursued their material and sexual lusts incited by the foreign gods and idols of Jezebel. As the wicked and ruthless wife of apostate King Ahad, Jezebel had offered Israel only that which lasts for a moment in exchange for that which lasts forever.

Trading instant pleasure for long-term pain, the people of Israel had flocked to worship pagan idols that could neither hear their petitions nor answer their prayers. But in the midst of this vain pursuit after gods who could not deliver—a similar state exists in today's culture—the people of Israel had grown tired of the magic of religious performance that produced only silence.

So a crowd gathered on Mount Carmel to watch a contest between the prophets of false religion and a sole representative of the true God, a prophet named Elijah. What transpired reveals much about finding God's presence, being still, and listening to his voice.[4]

Listening for the voice that does not exist. The prophets of religious immediacy gathered to call upon the name of their many imposter gods. They danced and shouted throughout the day, asking their gods to rain fire upon their altar as a dramatic message for their blinded, numbed followers. The ancient scene they created has been mimicked throughout the ages by false prophets and religious performers.

A crowd, not a people. Crowds and performances depend on one another. Like Siamese twins joined at the heart, it's impossible to have a true performance without a crowd. The performer sells his heart to the crowd and depends on it to pump life into his performance. And as soon as the crowd is surgically separated from the performance, the performer dies and the crowd disperses.

Like the followers of the false gods, you will be tempted to pursue God's presence where the masses flock. But contrary to the popular democratic opinion that the voice of the people is the voice of God, spiritual truth reveals God's voice may simply be that of a solitary prophet crying in the wilderness. The crowd is fickle; when dissatisfied, they quickly seek another performance, another emotional high, another momentary, heart-stopping, pulpit-pounding message that motivates the senses but fails to penetrate the heart.

A show, not an encounter. The false prophets perform, but their lifeless gods have no power to manifest. There comes a time when—exposed for what it truly is—religion cannot produce any kind of fruit. Like junk food, religious performances temporarily fill, but cannot give long-term nourishment.

You may have felt the momentary presence of God in a worship service, but even when genuine, his presence doesn't abide in temples built by hands.[5] So after the service, you may have felt empty, alone, and abandoned. What happened?

You are the temple and his Spirit desires to indwell you.[6] Corporate worship may invite God's presence and true worshippers may create an atmosphere for encountering his presence, but only your sincere heart seeking him can become the permanent dwelling place for God's presence.

It's hard for me to listen for God's voice when

_____

_____

_____

Back to Elijah and the false prophets. No matter how hard the prophets tried and performed, they could not conjure up that which did not exist. They danced and yelled but nothing happened to change them, their crowd, or the atmosphere around them.

At the end of the day, spent and exhausted, the false prophets retreated from the scene, leaving only a single, stubborn man who had but one advantage—Elijah had heard God's voice. He was the right person, in the right place, doing the right thing, not because he had planned it, but because he had found God's presence and heard God's voice.

Presence demonstrated with power. Acquainted with God's voice and obeying it, Elijah did everything to demonstrate to the crowd that it was God and not him who would show up. The true God would rain down fire upon the altar, Elijah promised. Elijah had servants pour water from twelve water pots upon the altar made of twelve stones. Then Elijah did a remarkable thing—he simply prayed. He talked with God. Refusing to speak to and mesmerize the crowd, Elijah appealed to an audience of one—God.

When finding a mentor to help you in the pursuit of God, look first to those who talk more with God than speak at man. Look for someone who tries to please God more than impress men. Find those who are just as comfortable sharing the power of his presence with a few as with a multitude.

Addressing God rather than the crowd, Elijah calmly and quietly called upon the name of his close friend—Someone who was real and present. Instead of seeking the endorsements of the notable, Elijah cared only about the approval of the One who will be present long after the notables have moved away.

So Elijah spoke to God and fire rained down from heaven, consuming the altar. The people cried out and acknowledged that God was truly God. Interestingly enough, however, the power failed to change them. The manifested power of God always invokes and inspires awe, wonder, fear, and amazement. But only abiding in his presence can produce permanent change within us.

If you seek God only for his power, if a manifestation of his glorious strength is all you desire, then no lasting change will happen within you and no residue of his presence will indwell you.

In the silence, God speaks. After the impressive service on Mount Carmel, Jezebel's prophets were killed by the crowd, as one might have anticipated. But Jezebel was still alive and angry with the lone ranger of God. So she ordered him killed.

Fleeing for his life, Elijah ran to the hills and hid in a cave. Pitying himself as the only true seeker and worshipper of God, Elijah sat alone in his depression and blamed God for his dismal fate.

Suddenly, more power manifested itself; earthquakes, wind, and fire shook and battered the prophet. As soon as they arrived, they departed. This time, no crowd, no miracles, no wonders, and no fireworks remained. Elijah stood alone in the resulting silence, listening for God's voice. Only after all the noise and chaos passed did Elijah hear God's voice—a quiet whisper. Elijah then began to understand that when every other voice and experience is silenced, then and only then can the still, small voice of God be heard.[7]

God speaks. Are you listening? What voices need to be silenced so you can hear his voice? More important, what inner idols vie for your spirit's attention? The flesh wars against the Spirit within you to keep you focused on everything but God. Especially distracting from his presence are all the religious performances around you that beckon you to do something, give something, change something, or center on something rather than God's still, small voice, speaking to your depths and desiring to occupy your center so that nothing or no one else can be in you. God whispers, "Be still, and know that I am God."

At the center of my being, I am still and listening to God's voice telling me to

_____

_____

_____

KEYS TO INVITING GOD'S PRESENCE

- Examine the center of your being. What occupies your center? (Circle all that apply.)

    God   Goals   Purpose

    Work   Possessions   Other people

    Other _____

- Are you willing to cast off anything in your center that is not of God?

- How do you handle listening? Does your listening require you to play music or have another activity happening instead of simply listening? Describe how you listen to God's voice.

    _____

    _____

    _____

- How do you hear the voice of God most clearly? (Circle one.)

    Circumstances   Scripture   Prayer

    Worship   Singing   Praise

    Silence   Others speaking to me about him

    Other _____

🔑 What new step will you take to listen more intensely for God's voice?

_____

_____

_____

———— ∞∞∞ ————

*Entering God's presence requires us to silence
competing voices in order to hear his.*

DAY 2

Hear and Obey

LISTENING WITHOUT OBEDIENCE FAILS TO INVITE God's presence. Faith without obedience fills a relationship with words unaccompanied by action. Without action, faith is dead and listening is meaningless.

So what if God speaks when you're in his presence and you don't hear and obey? Hearing implies obedience. When my wife asks or tells me to do something and I nod with the accompanying comment, "I hear you," she correctly assumes I will act upon what I have heard. And my response obligates me. Otherwise, our relationship has no accountability.

When Israel heard the commands of God but did not obey, God's rebuke was, "But they did not obey nor incline their ear, but made their neck stiff, that they might not hear nor receive instruction."[8] Hearing God's voice comes with a mandate—to obey.

The quickest exit from God's presence comes through disobedience. Disobedience reveals a rebellious heart that doesn't truly seek to abide in his presence. A striking example of obedience can be found in the story of a monk who was told to plant a dry stick in the sand and to water it daily.

> *So distant was the spring from his cell that he had to leave in the evening to fetch the water, and he only returned the following morning. For three years he patiently fulfilled his abba's command. At the end of this period, the stick suddenly put forth leaves and bore fruit. The abba picked the fruit, took it to the church, and invited the monks to eat, saying, "Come and taste the fruit of obedience."[9]*

Obedience produces something of worth—good fruit. Without obeying, hearing is fruitless. Jesus tells the story of a father with two sons. The man told the older boy, "Son, go out and work on the farm today."

"I won't," he answered, but later he changed his mind and went.

Then the father told the youngest, "You go!" and he said, "Yes, sir, I will." But he didn't.

Which of the two was obeying his father?"[10]

Obedience begins with listening. Listening proceeds with understanding. Hearing is:

➤ Being still in order to listen

➤ Silencing every other voice to hear the voice of God's presence

➤ Understanding what is heard

➤ Dialoguing with God

➤ Communing with God

➤ Obeying God's voice

➤ Bearing the fruit of obedience

I find it difficult to hear and obey when

_____

_____

_____

The voice of God's presence speaks through:

➤ Circumstances, dreams, and visions that he interprets

➤ Scripture, understood through his Spirit

➤ Prayers that dialogue with God: both of us speaking; both of us listening

➤ Other people who consistently speak truth in love into our lives

Hearing and obeying takes effort; it's not easy. Some desire to enter God's presence and then experience a life of effortless ease where prayers are easily answered, commands easily obeyed, and fruit easily grown. Is that how it is? Not exactly!

Abiding in God's presence doesn't come with cruise control. Cruise control makes obeying the speed limit on an interstate highway an easy thing. But remove the cruise control and one has to constantly check the speedometer.

When others go faster than us, we are encouraged to disobey. We rationalize, "They're disobeying. Why can't I?"

Or we find ourselves running late for an important meeting. We push the pedal to the metal believing that being on time (even though we started late) outweighs obedience.

Or we purchase a radar detector believing that not getting caught is the same as obedience.

Abiding in God's presence requires constantly checking with him on the directions and limits of life. Often we resist, preferring independence over accountability. Inviting and finding God's presence may have been tough, but abiding in his presence is even more difficult. The quest that we believed would make life easier has in fact confronted us with responsibilities and demands we never had before. Outside of his presence, we could do what we wanted. In his presence, we can only do what he wants.

In God's presence I

_____

_____

_____

Our life of hearing and obeying is epitomized in this verse: "And I know his instructions lead to eternal life; so whatever he tells me to say, I say!"[11] Of every word, ask, "Is that what I heard God tell me to say?" Of every action, ask, "Is that what I heard God tell me to do?"

KEYS TO INVITING GOD'S PRESENCE

⚷ Rank in order the ways that you hear God's voice, from most often to least often.

_____ Circumstances, dreams, and visions that he interprets

_____ Scripture understood through his Spirit

_____ Prayers that dialogue with God: both of us speaking; both of us listening

_____ Other people who consistently speak truth in love into our lives

---

When you hear God and don't obey, how does that affect your abiding in his presence?

_____

_____

_____

Thank God for all the benefits that come from hearing and obeying his voice.

———∞∞∞———

Abiding in God's presence requires hearing
and *obeying his voice.*

DAY 3

Let Go and Draw Near

Draw near to God and God will draw near to you.[12] Such intimacy requires that we leave something behind in order to grasp something new. Through the prophet Isaiah, God spoke about forgetting and leaving behind the past in order to perceive the new thing He is doing.[13] The apostle Paul indicates that for the new person to emerge from within us, the old must pass away.[14] To receive what is new, changed and refreshed, we need to grasp a willingness to let go of the past.

The past can never determine our future. To let something go is to leave it behind. Stories of how people enter God's presence often involve leaving something behind in order to step freshly and newly into God's leading presence. He goes before us as a pillar of cloud by day and a pillar of fire by night, leading us into a new thing: "Behold, I am doing a new thing. Do you not perceive it?" God asks.[15]

New means change and freshness. But to encounter the newness of God's presence, we must leave some things behind, as seekers of his presence have always discovered.

Abram and Sarai had to leave Ur behind to follow his presence.

The nation of Israel had to leave Egypt behind to follow God's presence into the wilderness.

- ➤ Joshua had to leave behind the wilderness.

- ➤ Ruth had to leave behind her homeland and family.

- ➤ Samuel had to leave Saul behind.

- ➤ Esther had to leave security behind.

- ➤ Peter, James, and John had to leave their boats and jobs behind.

- Jesus had to leave behind the cross and the tomb.

- Saul had to leave the Sanhedrin behind.

- Constantine had to leave the gods of Rome behind.

- Joan of Arc had to leave safety behind.

- Martin Luther had to leave tradition behind.

- John Wycliffe had to leave his church behind.

- The pilgrims had to leave Europe behind.

- Abraham Lincoln had to leave slavery behind.

- Martin Luther King Jr. had to leave the emotional bonds of discrimination behind.

What must I leave behind so I may continue on?

_____

_____

_____

To let go is to get up and go on. John Maxwell is quoted as saying, "To go up you must get up." Likewise, to go on in God's presence you must get up from where you are. Where you are may be comfortable and stable. Where you are may feel safe and secure. Where you are may be satisfying and fulfilling. But you can't sit where you are if you are to go on in God's presence.

- A lame man had to get up to receive healing.

- A blind man had to reach out to receive sight.

- A bleeding woman had to push through to become whole.

- A crazed demoniac had to come from the tombs to become sane.

Are you willing to get up and go on in God's presence?

The presence you've experienced in the past isn't enough to carry you on into your destiny. The presence you've encountered is like manna in the desert. It's good for the present, but spoils when carried into tomorrow.

My destiny in life is

_____

_____

_____

If you are lying around, paralyzed in depression, fatigue, and doubt, get up. Entering into God's presence requires truth or faith. Before you can go on, you must trust his voice, which says, "Follow me."

If you're lying around in your past sin, guilt, shame, and bondage, get up. Getting up requires turning away from sin and turning toward God. Let go and get up!

To let go means to surrender control. One of the most difficult aspects about being in God's presence is recognizing who's in control. As long as you are in control, God isn't. And as long as God isn't, you're not in his presence. Surrendering control means letting go of, "No, Lord," and constantly saying, "Yes, Lord." _No_ and _Lord_ are impossible to utter in the same sentence. If you say no, then he's not Lord.

God's presence goes where he chooses, not where we choose. Consequently, you may find yourself in new territory, uncharted waters, crossing over new horizons. So be it. Let go. Surrender all—not just some—to God's presence.

So, in God's presence, we let go of the past, get up from present circumstances, and surrender control of the future to God.

KEYS TO INVITING GOD'S PRESENCE

⚷ Describe the hardest thing for you to let go of.

_____

_____

_____

⚷ Complete the following:

I must leave behind

_____

I must get up and go on from

_____

I must surrender total control to God by

_____

🔑 Complete the following:

When I leave behind the past, I feel

_____

When I face the new thing of the future, I feel

_____

🔑 Reflect on any negative feelings about releasing the past. Why do you feel negative?

_____

_____

_____

🔑 Reflect on any negative feelings about embracing God's new future. Why do you feel negative?

_____

_____

_____

⸺❮❮❮⸺

In God's presence, we must let go, get up,
and surrender control to him.

DAY 4

Abide Intimately

ABIDING IS DIFFERENT THAN COHABITATION. When many people cohabitate, they often live together for the purpose of sex, not love. The purpose of their relationship focuses on pleasure and convenience instead of commitment and fruitfulness. Living together means that if one of the partners gets tired of the relationship, it's over; the partners go their separate ways.

Finding God's presence, inviting his presence, and remaining in his presence has nothing to do with cohabitation. Abiding in God's presence can be compared to marriage as opposed to cohabitation. Abiding is about:

➢ Endurance

➢ Commitment

➢ Trust

➢ Intimacy

➢ Fruitfulness

The hardest part of abiding is

_____

_____

_____

Endurance. "To abide" comes from an Old English word *bīdan*, whose contemporary rendition is *bide*. Its root connection, from German and Latin origins, means to believe and trust, which we will consider momentarily. Another root connection in the Greek means to remain current.

Abiding speaks of a daily, fresh experience in God's presence. Abiding also moves a relationship with God from temporary to enduring, out of the present into the future, and beyond convenience to commitment. Abiding that endures is steeled with patience, perseverance, and persistence. Even when doubt or silence threatens abiding, the abider waits with faith and listens throughout the silence. Abiding that endures discovers that commitment means a refusal to give up or abandon the relationship.

Commitment. Commitment gives security to a relationship. Commitment says, "I will be home tonight and will not sleep with another." Commitment also says, "I will be committed to you indefinitely."

Originally, *commitment* meant to put together, join, or connect. This evolved into the understanding that commitment entrusts and perpetuates. Abiding in God's presence, we experience a connection with him, a joining with his person, and a togetherness that feels safe, secure, and lasting.

God doesn't withdraw his presence just because we fail or disappoint him. Instead, God chooses to work in relationship with us to help us grow in our commitment. His presence brings to the relationship truth spoken in love and discipline that corrects. His presence lifts us from failure into success.

Trust. Abiding intimately in God's presence requires truth. We trust each other with everything—thoughts, feelings, and actions. We share everything. Trust means we can tell God anything without being rejected, abandoned, or hurt.

That doesn't mean that trust denies the truth. Our thoughts, feelings, and actions need to be examined by his standard of truth. Just because we think, feel, or act a certain way doesn't mean those thoughts or feelings reflect truth or that the action we've taken is right. But in God's presence, we can trust him to tell us the truth even when we cannot tell ourselves the truth: "But when he, the Spirit of truth, comes, he will guide you into all truth."[16]

Intimacy. Remember that abiding speaks of being connected and joining with another. This intimacy in God's presence is like marital intimacy. There is a joining together in love and closeness that become precious, holy, and eternal. The interaction between God's presence and us comes out of a deep, pure love. Jesus described intimate abiding this way: "As the Father loved Me, I also have loved you; abide in My love. If you keep My commandments, you will abide in My love, just as I have kept My Father's commandments and abide in His love."[17]

Fruitfulness. The end result of intimate abiding is producing fruit that lasts. "Abide in Me," Jesus said, "and I in you. As the branch cannot bear fruit of itself, unless it abides in the vine, neither can you, unless you abide in Me."[18] The fruit that comes out of intimate abiding will be our next discussion.

Intimate abiding takes time. Without time, no relationship can grow and deepen.

How do I spend time in God's presence?

_____

_____

_____

KEYS TO INVITING GOD'S PRESENCE

⚷ Look over your daily schedule. Find times when you can be intimate with God through worship, prayer, Scripture, study, contemplation, meditation, service, or giving. Write down the most intimate experience you have had with God recently.

_____

_____

_____

⚷ Share in God's presence with a friend who is also seeking and finding God's presence. What is your friend learning about God? What can you share with your friend about your experiences in God's presence?

_____

_____

_____

⚷ What keeps you from being intimate with God? Share those hindrances as you commune and dialogue with him.

———— ⸸ ————

God's presence invites you into abiding intimacy.

Bearing Fruit

EARLIER YOU READ THAT BEING IN GOD'S PRESENCE changes us. Much of that change begins within us—in our character. In his presence, we bear fruit, becoming more like God's character and nature. His abiding Spirit within us produces character that's loving, joyful, peaceful, patient, kind, good, loyal (faithful), gentle, and self-controlled.[19]

Love. Love seeks the best in another without expecting a return. We love, desiring God's best for another person. We love without expecting others to return our love. We give the gift of love without expecting that gift to be returned in kind. The classic definition of love is:

> *Love is patient, love is kind. It does not envy, it does not boast, it is not proud. It is not rude, it is not self-seeking, it is not easily angered, it keeps no record of wrongs. Love does not delight in evil but rejoices with the truth. It always protects, always trusts, always hopes, always perseveres. Love never fails.*[20]

Joy. Joy goes far beyond happiness. Happiness is always tied to happenstance. In other words, happiness is contingent upon good circumstances or good people coming into our lives. But joy isn't tied to externals. Joy is rooted in God's presence. Abiding in his presence produces inner joy regardless of life's ups and downs.

"Life is one long joy, because the will of God is always being done in it, and the glory of God is always being got from it."[21]

What is the difference for me between happiness and joy?

_____

_____

_____

Peace. We desire peaceful surroundings and relationships. Our natural inclinations lead many of us to avoid conflict and seek harmonious situations at almost any cost. But peace, like joy, is not dependent upon what's happening around us. Conflicts may abound and outer turmoil may engulf us; peace abides in his indwelling presence.

Inner peace arrives when the war between our selves and God's presence ceases. No longer at enmity with God, having torn down the walls between us and him, we can live at peace within ourselves.

"So now, since we have been made right in God's sight by faith in his promises, we can have real peace with him because of what Jesus Christ our Lord has done for us."[22]

Patience. Abiding in God's presence changes our impatient demanding, which we often misname *prayer,* into expectant waiting on God to speak and act. Patience is neither withdrawal nor inaction. We still hear and obey God's voice. We still move forward into his future. When we are patient, we involve ourselves with what God is doing instead of anxiously trying to force God into what we are doing.

Patience empowers us to move within his plan rather than to impatiently make our plans work. God's presence enables us to endure until the end instead of trying to end what we need to endure. Any momentary discomfort, pain, stress, or struggle that we patiently endure helps us to abide and remain in his presence.

We can rejoice, too, when we run into problems and trials, for we know that they are good for us—they help us learn to be patient. And patience develops strength of character in us and helps us trust God more each time we use it until finally our hope and faith are strong and steady.[23]

Kindness and goodness. Being kind and good to others arises from experiencing his kindness and goodness to us. At last, someone cherishes us for who we are and not for what we do. At last, we are given good gifts by the one who gives us every good and perfect gift.

Kindness moves from being a choice to becoming a mandate in our lives. We are kind because our nature and character necessitate kindness irrespective of the words or actions of another. We are good not because others are good to us but because the goodness of God's presence abides within us.

Loyalty (faithfulness). Being in the presence of a promise keeper helps us become promise keepers. We discover how to be trustworthy because God is trustworthy. "If God is for us, who can be against us?"[24]

Loyalty for us begins within family, expressed in covenant marriage and healthy family relationships. Loyalty extends to the workplace and our faith community. It's not a blind loyalty but rather a genuine commitment that says in all of our relationships, "You can count on me to be there for you; to keep my word; to treat you with mercy and grace; and to be a sincere friend."

Gentleness. Gentleness demonstrates itself in humility and servanthood. This attitude conforms to the servant attitude that Christ had toward others.[25] Such gentleness has strength, firmness, assertiveness, and boldness while still being kind, gracious, and serving. Gentleness seeks no glory or adulation for anything said or done. Its greatest reward comes through seeing another person encouraged, helped or edified.

Self-Control. Being responsible for our feelings and actions is a strong indicator of this fruit. Instead of being reason-driven or emotion-driven in life, we become presence-driven. When driven by God's presence, we discover that our ways yield to his. Driven by our own desires and wants, we often find ourselves moving from God's presence into selfish and worldly interests that have no power to restrain us or temper our excesses.

Abiding in God's presence produces fruit in our lives.

What fruit in my character do I currently see being produced?

_____

_____

_____

How is that fruit changing both me and my relationships?

_____

_____

_____

Examine the fruit in your life. Circle those that are growing and box those that need to grow. Spend time in God's presence asking him to empower and inspire you in ways that grow fruit in your life.

Love   Joy   Peace

Patience   Kindness   Goodness

Loyalty   Gentleness   Self-control

Take time to abide in God's presence. Allow competing voices to be silenced. Then do some of the following:

- Thank God for the fruit of his Spirit in your life
- Listen to how God affirms his love for you
- Seek God's direction for input on your future
- Ask God about his good plans for you

In your relationships with your spouse, child, parent, or close friend, what fruits do you see growing and how? How are the fruits revealed?

_____

_____

_____

⊸⊶⊷

Abiding in God's presence
produces lasting fruit.

Listening and Abiding in God's Presence

For me to listen to God, I must

_____

_____

_____

What I hear God saying to me is

_____

_____

_____

In drawing near to God, I

_____

_____

_____

Abiding intimately with God is

_____

_____

_____

In my life, the fruit of abiding in God's presence can best be observed when

_____

_____

_____

⊶⊷

Comforted and Loved Unconditionally in God's Presence

What matters supremely, therefore, is not, in the last analysis, the fact that I know God, but the larger fact which underlies it—that He knows me. I am graven on the palms of his hands. I am never out of His mind. All my knowledge of Him depends on His sustained initiative in knowing me. I know Him because he first knew me, and continues to know me.

He knows me as a friend, one who loves me; and there is no moment, therefore, when His care falters. This is momentous knowledge.

There is unspeakable comfort . . . in knowing that God is taking knowledge of me in love and watching over me for my good.

There is tremendous relief in knowing that His love is utterly realistic, based at every point on prior knowledge of the worst about me, so that no discovery can disillusion Him about me, in the way I am so often disillusioned about myself, and quench His determination to bless me.

—J. I. PACKER,
KNOWING GOD

Introduction

WHAT A COMFORT IT IS TO BE UNDERSTOOD BY ANOTHER person. Whenever we hurt, God understands our pain and discomfort. When we suffer, the balm of his compassion soothes and eases our burdens.

Abiding in God's presence brings us the comfort we need in the most critical crises of life. Perhaps the greatest ailment we face was labeled by Søren Kierkegaard as *angst*—a generalized gloom, depression, and anxiety over the future. Certainly depression could be called the psychological AIDS of our time. While much depression goes unreported, estimates are that over 17 million Americans suffer from depression and that 90 percent of all suicides are related to depression.[1] Many agree that depression is the number one ailment facing our culture.

Depression and anxiety. When we feel depressed and anxious, gloomy and worried about the future, God's presence comforts us. Constantly listening to the news and reading about events around us, we can easily become depressed. All the news seems to be bad and the future of everything from the stock market to social mores seems to be gloomy. Without God's presence, we could become lost in the morass of angst.

In God's presence, comfort exists that will lift us up from these doom-and-gloom feelings and will restore hope and faith. As Kierkegaard affirms, "Man is capable of nothing. It is God who gives everything, who gives man faith."

Fear and dread. Fear has become a primary paralysis in many lives. We fear tomorrow and what it may bring—financial losses, death, pain, disease, attack, or persecution. We fear what others may do to us or say about us. We fear what may happen to our children. Fear becomes a primary motivator in many of our relationships. We react with fear instead of faith when facing life's problems and challenges.

In God's presence, fear melts away like ice left exposed to a scorching, hot sun on a midsummer's day. Fear cannot exist in God's presence.

Suffering and pain. For centuries the debate about a good and loving God allowing his children to suffer has raged. Truthfully, we cannot endure pain and suffering without God's presence. God's presence isn't an escape clause for us to bypass tribulations in life. His presence does give us the strength and ability to go through any "valley of shadows" that looms ahead.

Adam and Eve's departure from God's presence birthed humanity into a world of suffering and pain. Out of rebellion and self-centeredness came separation, brokenness, evil, and suffering.

Suffering is of the essence of life, because it is the inevitable product of an unresolved tension between a living creature's essential impulse to try to make itself into the centre of the Universe and its essential dependence on the rest of Creation and on the Absolute reality.[2]

While there remains mystery in the problem of suffering that defies complete human understanding, an even greater mystery exists for us: God chooses to participate in our suffering. God chooses to walk with us through suffering and pain that he did not author. "If thou can be still and suffer awhile, thou shalt without doubt see the help of God come in thy need."[3]

Seeking love. All the while that we are pursuing God, inviting his presence, and entering into his presence, God is pursuing us. Ever present, always caring, ever reaching, God meets us with outstretched arms as a father welcoming home a lost son. His presence was always available and awaiting our decision to tear down the walls so that we might turn away from separation, guilt, rebellion, pain, or whatever idol kept us away and turn to the presence of the lover of our souls.

For the Christian, God's participation in our suffering and his unconditional love for us is best understood while standing in the shadow of a cross and seeing him die for us. "Greater love has no one than this, than to lay down one's life for his friends."[4] Those who would profess to be religious have made religion, including Christianity, a precondition for receiving God's love and encountering his presence. Yet just the opposite is true: "He loved us ere we knew him."[5]

Unconditional love. As we have experienced in the post-September 11 world, our pursuit of God may be least abetted by religion. In the name of religion, men hated and destroyed. And in the name of religion, other men reacted angrily while striking back with prejudice, profiling, persecution, and vengeance. As social critic and satirist Jonathan Swift observed, "We have just enough religion to make us hate, but not enough to make us love one another."

It is not religion that brings us into God's presence. Rather God invites; we acknowledge his invitation and respond to it. "Love is union with somebody, or something, outside oneself, under the condition of retaining separateness and integrity of one's self."[6]

Before we knew how to love; before we became aware of being loved; before we changed and moved out from behind our walls; before we turned away from the past, guilt, shame, or selfishness; before we understood that One was there for us; before we felt or knew about God's presence, he loved us with a seeking, searching, unconditional love. In his presence, by his love, through our response of faith and trust, we are changed from one lost to one found by love.

This week you will discover that in God's presence his comfort abounds toward you and strengthens you to face any trial, test, or tribulation. You will experience in God's presence the unconditional love of One who understands your grief and knows your sorrow.

Comfort for Depression and Anxiety

D EPRESSION CAN AFFLICT THE LEAST AND THE greatest in society. No one can be forever immunized from loss out of which comes depression. But depression can become indigenous with our inner selves when we respond to loss with anger and bitterness instead of awareness and recognition that we need help and comfort from another. Dr. M. Scott Peck observes:

> *Since mentally healthy human beings must grow, and since giving up or loss of the old self is an integral part of the process of mental and spiritual growth, depression is a normal and basically healthy phenomenon. It becomes abnormal or unhealthy only when something interferes with the giving-up process, with the result that the depression is prolonged and cannot be resolved by completion of the process.*[7]

Giving up the old. Some are surprised when they enter God's presence to discover the paradox of joy laced with grief or depression. The joy of friendship with the One who loves us comes with the price of tearing down walls that we neurotically or erringly believed protect us from grief. Existence feels no pain, only numbness. But life imparted in his presence exposes us to all kinds of loss, grief, pain, and suffering.

What of the past is hardest for me to release?

_____

_____

_____

Outside of God's presence, we can harden our hearts and ignore both the misery of others and ourselves simply by saying, "Everyone gets what they deserve." But in his presence, we become empathetic and vulnerable to loss—both our own and the loss experienced by others.

Inviting God's presence brings us to the realization that a heart of stone that feels no pain has been replaced by a heart of flesh—a heart that is vulnerable, sensitive, compassionate, and empathetic.

Then I will give them one heart, and I will put a new spirit within them, and take the stony heart out of their flesh, and give them a heart of flesh, that they may walk in My statutes and keep My judgments and do them; and they shall be My people, and I will be their God.[8]

Growing in his presence, we come to understand we have lost the old self and are becoming a new person. *The Message* describes it this way: "Now we look inside, and what we see is that anyone united with Messiah gets a fresh start, is created new. The old life is gone; a new life burgeons! Look at it! All this comes from the God who settled the relationship between us and him and then called us to settle our relationships with each other."[9]

Giving up the old self, the stony heart, and receiving new life actualizes within us, in a new and profound way, the ability to grieve over the pain we cause and the pain others both experience and cause. No longer do I shed tears for myself because I experience the floodgates of God's tears shed for me. Instead, I begin to grieve for what I have done to myself and others out of a stony heart. And I grieve for others who hurt within and hurt others—hurting people hurting others.

Healthy depression arising from such real loss enables us to turn to God for comfort.

You let the distress bring you to God, not drive you from him. The result was all gain, no loss. Distress that drives us to God does that. It turns us around. It gets us back in the way of salvation. We never regret that kind of pain. But those who let distress drive them away from God are full of regrets, ending up on a deathbed of regrets.[10]

Overcoming the grief of depression in a flood of tears. Don't waste your tears. Save them as a soothing balm to dress the wounds of others. Having acknowledged our losses and been comforted in his presence, we can then comfort others.

In worship services at my church, the presence of God fills and overflows us. Many newcomers to this type of worship shed buckets of tears for weeks, sometimes months, on end. Even after the initial season of experiencing God's presence, the tears easily and quickly flow in worship, prayer, and entering into intimacy with God. Many ask, "Why do I cry so much in God's presence?"

You may find yourself asking the same question. Take comfort in your tears. "Blessed are those that mourn for they shall be comforted."[11] Behind our walls and apart from God's presence, we deny our grief, bury our sorrow, and repress our pain. But in his presence, we lose the old self and mourn. "You are blessed when you feel you have lost what's most dear to you. Only then can you be embraced by the one most dear to you."[12]

In his presence, we are quickly convicted whenever a part of our new heart is tempted to become stone again, and we grieve.

In his presence, we feel the pain and loss that is experienced and caused by others, and we grieve.

In his presence, we discover that depression, grief, and sorrow are overcome by comforting others with the comfort his presence affords you. To the ancient residents of Corinth, Paul the Apostle wrote of God's comforting presence:

> *"He comes alongside us when we go through hard times, and before you know it, he brings us alongside someone else who is going through hard times so that we can be there for that person just as God was there for us.*
>
> *"We have plenty of hard times that come from following the Messiah, but no more so than the good times of his healing comfort—we get full measure of that, too."*[13]

Beyond angst. Are we anxious about what will happen to us? Or is it that we are anxious about having to face what will happen to us alone? We can face almost anything knowing we don't have to walk into it or through it by ourselves.

A woman faces the anxiety and pain of childbirth with comfort knowing that her husband will be at her side, breathing with her and encouraging her through the pain. A spouse anxiously faces the impending death of a terminally ill mate knowing the comfort of a helper from hospice is there. A patient rolls down the hospital corridor toward a surgery suite clutching the hand of a friend who prays for healing and imparts assurance and strength.

We are comforted in God's presence. "And why does he do this? So that when others are troubled, needing our sympathy and encouragement, we can pass on to them this same help and comfort God has given us."[14]

Who and how am I comforting with the tears and comfort I have received from being in God's presence?

_____

_____

_____

KEYS TO INVITING GOD'S PRESENCE

- Seek out a homeless shelter, a nursing home, a hospital ward, an urban mission center, a daycare center for the elderly, or some other place where comfort is needed. Go there to comfort others. Experience in your going the presence of God.

- Enter his presence. Allow your tears to flow—tears of grief over what you were that must be lost in order to become all that you are in God's presence. Let another weep with you, and then weep with them.

- Don't worry about tomorrow. Instead give your cares to God when you enter his presence. Meditate on this: "Cast all your anxiety on him because he cares for you."[15]

In God's presence we are comforted and,
in turn, comfort others.

Conquering
Fear and Dread

T HE ONE WHO COMFORTS US GIVES US THE COURAGE and strength to announce in the face of all that reality throws at us: "No fear!" Dread and fear of the future robs the present of joy, hope, and life itself.

Outside of his presence, we live in hopeless, comfortless fear. After all, anything could happen, we surmise. And endorsing Murphy's Law—if anything can go wrong, it will go wrong—we live anticipating the worst instead of hoping for the best.

What is it that we fear and dread? It comes down to three things: loss, pain, and death. We fear losing possessions and relationships. We fear experiencing pain or causing pain. We fear death. More specifically, we dread the pain we may go through in the midst of terminal disease, and we fear the unknown on the other side of death.

Conquering fear through God's loving presence. In counseling sessions, I sometimes ask people to imagine the worst scenario that might happen to them. God's presence empowers us to face the flight-or-fight syndrome that pumps adrenaline into us when we face real or imagined fears. Fleeing from our fears, we never move into the present and are always haunted by spirits of fear from the past that beat us then and threaten to attack and beat us again.

Fighting against our fears without God's presence only serves to remind us of how fragile and weak we are. The bravado we express when talking about the battle seems to vanish when we come face to face with "the enemy," whoever or whatever that foe may be.

I most fear

_____

_____

_____

However, in God's presence, every battle belongs to him. He fights *with* us and *for* us. When facing Goliath, David discovered the strengthening reality of God's presence: "All those gathered here will know that it is not by sword or spear that the Lord saves; for the battle is the Lord's, and he will give [Goliath and the Philistines] into our hands."[16] A. W. Tozer wrote in *Five Vows for Spirit Power* that one essential vow we should make is "Never defend yourself." Why defend ourselves when God is our sure defense?[17] Certainly he can do a much better job than we can!

In the midst of the battle, we discover God's presence also brings comforting friends to support us. As God's presence defeated the enemies of Israel, Moses interceded for God's people. Moses didn't have the strength to fight the battle nor the endurance to abide in God's presence while the battle raged. But comforting friends kept Moses in God's presence even when he lacked the strength to go on. When Moses' hands grew tired, his friends helped him to sit on a stone. Aaron and Hur held his arms up—one on one side, one on the other—so his hands remained steady till sunset. Joshua and the Israelites overcame the Amalekite army. Moses built an altar and called it The Lord Is My Banner. He said, "For hands were lifted up to the throne of the Lord. The Lord will be at war against the Amalekites from generation to generation."[18]

Ceasing from self-defense. We also become emotionally defensive when we fear losing our reputation, self-esteem, or honor. In God's presence, we have nothing to fear. Paul's ancient victory hymn can become ours:

For I am convinced that nothing can ever separate us from his love. Death can't, and life can't. The angels won't, and all the powers of hell itself cannot keep God's love away. Our fears for today, our worries about tomorrow, or where we are—high above the sky, or in the deepest ocean—nothing will ever be able to separate us from the love of God demonstrated by our Lord Jesus Christ when he died for us.[19]

Overcoming death's dread. God's presence surrounded us in the womb and will enshroud us through the grave. Death can extinguish existence; death cannot defeat life. God speaks life to us through the word of his indwelling presence. When we are present with God, we come face to face with his Word of life. That Word of life and light cannot be overcome by the darkness of death:

> *The Word was first,*
> *the Word present to God.*
> *God present to the Word.*
> *The Word was God,*
> *in readiness for God from day one.*
> *Everything was created through*
> *Him;*
> *nothing—not one thing!—*
> *came into being without him.*
> *What came into existence was Life,*
> *And the Life was the light to live by.*
> *The Light-Life blazed out of the*
> *darkness.*
> *The darkness couldn't put it out.*[20]

Death has no power over life. Our dread of death is replaced by the comforting assurance that God's presence prevails over the grave. God's presence in Christ defeated death once and for all. God's indwelling presence in us conquers our fear of death.

Before inviting God's presence, we existed in sin and separation from him. In his presence, we live in both time and eternity. As the apostle Paul wrote, "It was sin that made death so frightening and law-code guilt that gave sin its leverage, its destructive power. But now in a single victorious stroke of Life, all three—sin, guilt, death—are gone, the gift of our Master, Jesus Christ. Thank God!"[21]

With nothing to fear or dread, I will live my life

_____

_____

_____

⚷ Imagine your tombstone. What epitaph will be written on it? Will it be positive or negative—focused on ending or beginning, death or life? What epitaph would God write?

_____

_____

_____

⚷ In the midst of our fear and dread, Christ appears and says, "Fear not! What are you hiding from? What battle do you dread? Will you surrender your fear to God?" What is your response to him?

_____

_____

_____

⚷ Who do you need to hold up your arms as the battle rages? As God's presence fights for you, what friends do you have who will surround you with his comfort and love?

_____

_____

_____

⸺⸺⸺◎◎◎⸺⸺⸺

In God's presence, fear not!

DAY 3

Passing through Suffering and Pain

"WILL THE SUFFERING AND PAIN EVER END?" asked my beleaguered friend. I hesitated to speak the truth in love. "As long as existence battles life and the struggle between good and evil continues, suffering and pain will exist. But they will not prevail," I replied.

My friend took little comfort in my words because he allowed the fire of suffering to burn him instead of braze him. Like metal vases made harder, like clay pots fired in a hearth, we are instruments and vessels in his presence, being steeled to contain his fiery presence. My friend could not grasp this and so was uncomforted.

The whys of pain and suffering can never be fully explained by reason or emotion. But we can know with certainty that in the presence of God we are prepared and protected to weather the storm and sail most assuredly into safe harbor. Casting our sails to catch the wind of God's Spirit, we move forward into the future regardless of painful risk. Suffering makes us bitter or better depending on our response. In our own strength, we cannot endure.

I release the bitterness, pain, and suffering arising from

_____

_____

_____

Like brittle, unfired clay, we will snap under the stress of suffering and pain. But God has made a way through—not around—every trial, tribulation, and test.

His way is mysterious but nonetheless unchanging from age to age. It is one of the many things in God's dealing with us, that seems so very mysterious—that He should have made "suffering a condition of sanctity."[22]

Beyond the pain, we can experience deeper growth and intimacy with God, depending on how we respond. A speaker's comment once shocked me at first: "God cares more about how you respond than about what happens to you," he remarked. In my own desires, I want God to care about my circumstance. In reality, God cares about me more than my circumstance.

In every trial three elements are present—God's presence, the circumstance, and me. Two are unchanging—God and the circumstance. What happened, happened. No explanation—theological, existential, philosophical, or rational—can go back in time and space and change the circumstance.

Thank God, he is changeless. "Every good gift and every perfect gift is from above, and comes down from the Father of lights, with whom there is no variation or shadow of turning."[23] God simply says to us, "I am the Lord, I do not change."[24]

Suffering robs existence but cannot rob life of meaning. We have to choose how we will respond to suffering and how we will change with God's help. God's presence permeates even the most tragic situation with what Frankl terms optimism. After all, "saying yes to life in spite of everything," presupposes that life is potentially meaningful under any conditions, even those that are most miserable. And this in turn presupposes the human capacity to creatively turn life's negative aspects into something positive or constructive. In other words, what matters is to make the best of any given situation. "The best"—that which in Latin is called optimum—allows for: (1) turning suffering into a human achievement and accomplishment; (2) deriving from guilt the opportunity to change oneself for the better; and (3) deriving from life's transitoriness an incentive to take responsible action.[25]

Going through suffering, we change. In his presence, that change in us works for good. In fact, in every circumstance "God works for the good of those who are called according to his purpose and conformed to his presence."[26] We are being changed from glory to glory; we are growing from faith to faith; we are moving from deep to deep in relationship with God.

God's presence takes us through tribulation. God's presence isn't an escape hatch out of time's trials into eternity's bliss. His comforting presence takes us through every valley with a shadow of death as Psalm 23 declares: "Yea though I walk through the valley of the shadow of death, thou art with me. Thy rod and thy staff they comfort me."[27]

As masses of people descended through the fire and smoke down the stairs of the burning World Trade Center, one man testified that he heard others reciting the familiar words of Psalm 23. As I watched him tell his story to the camera, I marveled at his peace and calm in the midst of such a tragedy. Many of his coworkers and friends never made it out of the second tower before its collapse. The serene survivor told of how he learned the meaning of those words as he went through the crisis.

God's presence goes with us through the pain and suffering. In fact, God has participated in our sorrow and grief, our suffering and pain.

> *Surely he took up our infirmities*
> *and carried our sorrows,*
> *yet we considered him stricken by God,*
> *smitten by him, and afflicted.*
>
> *But he was pierced for our transgressions,*
> *he was crushed for our iniquities;*
> *the punishment that brought us peace was upon him,*
> *and by his wounds we are healed.*[28]

Living on the other side of the pain and suffering we find ourselves changed. "Pure gold put in the fire comes out of it proved pure; genuine faith put through suffering comes out proved genuine."[29]

God never leaves us or forsakes us. In going through, we are changed, refined, prepared, and made ready for the next trial that emerges. Without his presence, we would falter, fall, and fail. In his presence we pass through and emerge stronger. And if we stumble, we will not fall, "for the Lord upholds" us with his hand.[30]

I am healing from

_____

_____

_____

🔑 Examine the most painful trial, test, or tribulation you have faced alone in life. How did you respond? In what condition did you find yourself after it was over? Now examine the latest trial you have faced with God's presence. How did you respond? How were you changed?

_____

_____

_____

🔑 On a separate piece of paper, write down any bitter or angry feelings you have toward God about suffering and pain you have experienced. Read your words out loud to God. Invite his presence. Ask God to heal the hurt and comfort you in your pain. Set on fire and burn up what you have written. Meditate on this: "God is like a refiner's fire."[31]

🔑 Write a prayer thanking God for his comforting presence in your life.

_____

_____

_____

In God's comforting presence, suffering becomes
a refining fire changing us for the better.

God's Seeking Love

My children and I loved playing hide and seek. They would run away and hide as I counted to one hundred. Then I would slowly and loudly parade around the house or yard announcing my intention: "I'm going to find you. You can't hide from me forever." Their joyful laughter and giggling always betrayed their hiding place. After all, they wanted to be found and once found, they hungered to be tickled and rumbled with until all of us lay exhausted but fulfilled on the ground, too weak to tickle or laugh anymore.

For those outside his presence, God may seem to be a judging, stern curmudgeon who delights in punishing us. Nothing could be further from the truth. Like a loving father, God seeks us out when we are hiding or lost.

What three adjectives would I use to describe God the Father?

_____

_____

_____

There is no other blessing I can give you, no gift so precious, no treasure so refreshing, nothing that can more provision you for the journey we are all making, than to tell you that Someone is searching diligently for you. He is not a stationary God. He is crazy about you. The expense to which he has gone isn't reasonable, is it? The Cross was not a dignified ransom. To say the least, it was a splurge of love and glory lavishly spent on you and me:

> ➤ "While we were yet sinners, Christ died for the ungodly."

➤ "A shepherd having a hundred sheep, if he loses one, leaves the ninety-nine to go after the one and searches diligently until he finds it. God is like that shepherd. That is enough to make me laugh and cry."[32]

"We love because God first loved us."[33] He came into the darkness of our existence bringing the light of life—his presence. Struggling desperately to tear down the walls that separated us from him, we remove the last brick, ready to launch out and find him only to be surprised with the joy of realizing God had been right there all the time. He had been waiting, watching, seeking, and loving us.

Only God's faint whisper of love could penetrate our walls and echo through the thick doors of our hearts. Since we provided no key or entry code, God had no option but to knock until we open the door. The voice of his presence calls out to us: "Look at me. I stand at the door. I knock. If you hear me call and open the door, I'll come right in and sit down to supper with you."[34]

Frightened, lonely, hurting, and engulfed in darkened existence, we desperately search, knowing we can never find God's presence unless we are first found by the Light of his presence.

Our pursuit of God is successful just because He is forever seeking to manifest Himself to us. The revelation of God to any man is not God coming from a distance once upon a time to pay a brief and momentous visit to man's soul . . . There is no idea of physical distance involved in the concept. It is not a matter of miles, but of experience.[35]

Handicapped by all we have been and unable to become what we are intended to be, we find ourselves in a straight-jacket laced with the straps of failure, weakness, and selfishness. Exhausted by trying, confused by religious rules and regulations, frustrated by circumstances, and wounded by past hurts from friend and foe alike, we fall exhausted in our pursuit of God, believing we have reached the end prematurely and without having caught sight of the One for whom we search.

Lying face down in the mud of failure and futility, we envision ourselves as marathon runners who have almost reached the finish line but have just fallen short. Religious onlookers jeer and cry out, "Just a little more. You're almost there." But no matter how hard we try, we cannot go one inch further. Almost gleeful, the self-righteous denounce, condemn, and judge us with, "My, my, you've missed God."

And yet, looking up into what we expect to be an empty void, we glimpse a blurry visage through our tears of pain and failure. Face to face, we find God's presence. Before we fell, God had seen our race, felt our pain, carried our failure, and determined to bring the finish line to us. Rejoicing, God gathers us into his arms, holds us close, and whispers, "I have loved you with an everlasting love. Welcome home."

Unconditional, seeking love. Jessica has taught me more about God's seeking love than anyone I have ever known. I met Jessica when she was only three months old and weighed a meager six pounds. Her life epitomized the tragedy of innocent suffering and pain.

Jessica was born normal with one exception: she had no sucking reflex. Her single, unwed mother had four other children under the age of six when Jessica was born. In the hospital, the nurses and aides carefully taught Jessica's mother how to manipulate her jaws and lips to teach her how to suck. This took much time, patience, and effort. Everything worked well as long as Jessica and her mom were in the hospital. But upon returning back home, Jessica's mom was overwhelmed with all the tasks required now by the care of five children under the age of six, including Jessica, who couldn't suck properly and thus was forever hungry and crying.

This proved too much for Jessica's mom. She simply didn't have the time to teach baby Jessica how to suck. And she had no tolerance for her constant crying. As a result, whenever Jessica cried, she received a hard slap on the face to shut her up. This continued to the point where Jessica could no longer see or hear due to cerebral concussions. Jessica had also learned how to cry on the inside—trembling violently whenever she was hungry or touched.

By the time a social worker discovered Jessica's plight, she was almost dead. Saved by modern medical intervention, Jessica recovered in the hospital NICU unit until she could be fed with a tube by foster parents. My wife, Judi, and I became those parents. As a registered nurse in neonatal care with extensive nursery experience, Judi became the foster caregiver and I became the aide. Relieving my wife, I would feed Jessica during the night watches.

At first, when I went in to her room for her scheduled tube feeding, my initial touch of Jessica would prompt her to tremble violently with fear and to cry on the inside, never making an audible sound. Instead of cuddling, she remained rigid and frightened as I held her. She had never known the presence of another without accompanying pain.

For months I maintained the routine, going to Jessica night after night without any sign of a response other than fear and dread. I sang to her as I fed and rocked her. I knew she could feel the vibration of my songs in the night. I would softly speak to her of my love. Still, no response.

Then late one night, months after she first lay in my arms, when I picked her up, she didn't tremble with fear or cry in silence. In fact, she cuddled. She cooed. She received the touch and the hug that I offered her. She accepted my comforting and unconditional loving presence into her life.

Some of us are much like Jessica. God's unconditional loving, seeking presence reaches out to hold us, touch us, and comfort us. If we can but stop trembling in fear, crying in silence, and resisting his touch, we will be made whole in his presence. Though Jessica never saw my face physically, we met face-to-face in love and touched one another heart-to-heart.

Look up into God's loving face. Receive his healing touch. His presence hugs you with unconditional love and seeks to make you whole.

What keeps me from opening the door and letting God's loving presence heal me?

_____

_____

_____

KEYS TO INVITING GOD'S PRESENCE

⚿ Ask God to reveal to you the key that unlocks the door of your heart. Let his presence come in.

_____

_____

_____

⚿ When God's loving presence comes and touches you with healing, what do you experience?

_____

_____

_____

⚮ Identify your pain. Release your fear. Let go of your past. Hear God's voice. Receive unconditional love. Allow God's presence to hug you.

_____

_____

_____

———— ⚭ ————

Found by his presence, open yourself to
God's unconditional love.

Receiving and Giving Unconditional Love

THE RIVER OF GOD'S LOVING PRESENCE CANNOT simply flow into our lives without an outlet. The fresh water of the Jordan River flows into a stopped-up, enclosed sea—the Dead Sea. Nothing flows out, so all the fresh water is lost and that which could have sustained life is now a lifeless mire just existing in the middle of a desert.

God's presence isn't a lake or pond to be enjoyed only in the private moments of our own needs and wants. What's given is intended to be shared. "We love because he first loved us." If we fail to let the river of his presence flow through us and into the lives of others, we become dead, lifeless seas that contain only stale water and that never refresh.

"My dear, dear friends, if God loved us like this, we certainly ought to love each other. No one has seen God, ever. But if we love one another, God dwells deeply within us, and his love becomes complete in us—perfect love!"[36]

Someone in your life needs the healing touch of God's unconditional love just as desperately as you need it. Someone needs to hear good news, not just the world's bad news. Someone bound in fear needs to be released by God's perfect love. Someone who is hungry, thirsty, naked, imprisoned, lonely, or sick needs you to become the vessel that pours out the river of God's unconditional love into his or her life.

I allow God's presence to flow through me and touch others with his unconditional love by

_____

_____

_____

Consider taking these steps:

➤ Ask God to reveal to you someone who needs love

➤ Find someone who needs God's love but cannot love you in return. Give without expecting any return or response from them

➤ Choose an enemy and decide to show kindness to him or her

➤ Decide to forgive and love unconditionally your family members even before they repent

➤ Ask those whom you have hurt to forgive you

➤ Pray for those you know who may be hurting, sick, lonely, imprisoned, or impoverished

➤ Financially help someone in need without expecting to be repaid

➤ Visit someone who is sick or in prison

I will choose two things from the above list and I will follow through with them by

_____

_____

_____

This is not an exhaustive list but merely suggested first steps for reaching out with God's love. Love in the present. Don't procrastinate and put love off. What if that person dies before you tell them, "God loves you and so do I"?

Remember that God's presence is present; God is present to love you and others unconditionally right now. In the past, his love has sustained you. In the future, his love will meet you. But unconditional love is best expressed in the present, in the now!

I was regretting the past
And fearing the future . . .
Suddenly my Lord was speaking:
"My name is I Am." He paused.
I waited. He continued.

"When you live in the past,
with its mistakes and regrets,
it is hard. I am not there.
my name is not I Was.

"When you live in the future,
with its problems and fears,
it is hard. I am not there.
my name is not I Will Be.

"When you live in the moment,
it's not hard.
I am here.
My name is I Am."[37]

When we love "the least of these,"[38] we demonstrate our love of God. When we share God's unconditional love, we allow the river of his presence to flow through us and touch others. That is the river of life. There's healing, hope, and refreshing in the river of God's presence.

KEYS TO INVITING GOD'S PRESENCE

- Keep a daily journal of whom you are reaching out to with God's unconditional love. As you serve and minister to them, be open to God's presence flowing through you to touch them.

- Has God spoken to you about something to do or someone to love but you have procrastinated in responding? Write down what you need to do. Set a time to do it.

_____

_____

_____

Comforted and Loved Unconditionally in God's Presence   253

O—⚿ List people who have let the river of God's presence flow through them to you. Thank God for them and find ways to thank them for ministering his unconditional love to you.

———⟨⟩———

God's presence flows through you to
others as unconditional love.

Comforted and Loved Unconditionally in God's Presence

God's perfect love has overcome the spirit of fear in

_____

_____

_____

When I feel depressed, I discover in God's presence that

_____

_____

_____

In God's presence, my worries and anxieties

_____

_____

_____

I have experienced God's seeking love

_____

_____

_____

God has worked goodness into my suffering and pain through

_____

_____

_____

———————— ∞ ————————

The atmosphere of God's presence
is permeated with love.

Accepted and Forgiven in God's Presence

*Forgiveness is the answer to
the child's dream of a
miracle by which what is
broken is made whole
again, what is soiled is
again made clean.*

—DAG HAMMARSKJÖLD,
MARKINGS

Introduction

A CCEPTANCE AND BELONGING STRIKE DEEP CHORDS IN THE human soul. Teenagers hunger for acceptance so desperately that some cave into peer pressure even when it can destroy them or their families. Employees may do everything possible to be accepted by employers, even if employers ask for actions that violate the employees' values or mores.

At the root of acceptance is the answer to this probing question: Whom are you trying to please—God or man?

Entering into God's presence, we discover that God accepts us the way we are and then empowers us to please him and bless others. At the core of God's acceptance of us is the reality that we are forgiven. Nothing we do can earn forgiveness—it is a gift of grace. At the same time, God mandates us to forgive others or he will not forgive us. Forgiven in his presence, we can reach out to extend mercy and forgiveness to others.

Accepted and accepting others. In God's presence, prejudice disintegrates. I cannot judge others, for the right to judge is reserved for God alone. I can accept others because God accepts them. They don't have to change, clean up, straighten up, or get themselves right to be accepted by me. My acceptance of them as persons does not mean I accept their destructive or sinful attitudes, behaviors, or words. Acceptance extends to the person while discernment through God's presence is applied to their lifestyles.

Accepted and aiming to please. A colloquial expression from my homeland in Tennessee is, "I'm just aiming to please." So, what are we aiming at in God's presence? What's his priority for my purpose, direction, and mission in life? Since my acceptance cannot be jeopardized by any risk I take on his behalf, I am free to fail in man's eyes as long as I aim to please the only One who matters.

Accepted with favor and blessing. In God's presence, we find favor with God and with others. His blessing and prosperity fill our lives and overflow into the lives of others. Outside of God's presence, all we ultimately experience is problems, pain, need, and curses. We must decide where we want to live—in blessings or in curses.

Receiving mercy and forgiveness. In God's presence, we live in a continual state of mercy and grace. Through mercy, we don't receive what we have earned. Through grace, we receive what we cannot earn. When we live in God's presence, we continue to receive his mercy instead of judgment and wrath. We continue to experience his grace even though we cannot earn it.

Showing mercy and forgiveness. When others hurt us, we are tempted to slam them and hurt back. However, God's presence gives us the power and motivation to show mercy in spite of what an enemy or a friend does to us.

In God's presence, you will discover this week not only the good news of your acceptance, but also the source of power for accepting and forgiving others.

Accepted and Accepting Others

IN GOD'S PRESENCE, WE EXPERIENCE HIS ACCEPTANCE of us and he gives us the power to accept others. Outside of God's presence, we find ourselves judgmental and condemning of others. In his presence, we hear the important command, "Judge not, that you be not judged."[1] What we accept is the person, not necessarily the person's behavior. The following story truly represents the power of love over judgment.

In Nepal, we stood in the center of the largest underground church in the area. The missionary founder of this mother church stood next to us as our interpreter. At the end of the service, she began to speak in passionate terms in the native tongue of the region. We stood quietly, watching the faces before us transform from smiles to tears.

Suddenly, three men and a woman stood. Weeping, they rushed to the front of the room and fell on their faces in front of us. Perplexed, I asked the interpreter what she had said to incite such a response. She quietly explained that almost a year before, these four committed souls had traveled into an outlying, remote village more than a three-week bus ride from our present location. In that village they had planted a small church of about a dozen peasants. The small group had flourished for about ten months.

Then the Maoists had discovered their existence. They came to the village and burnt the small church to the ground. The four missionaries had been away at the time and heard of everything they owned being destroyed. Fearing for their lives, they fled back to the mother church. This weekend was the first time they had been back among their church family.

"Why are they here at the front?" I asked.

"They have come forward to repent for leaving their ministry post and not being willing to return and give up their lives for Christ."

By this point, all of us in attendance were weeping. With loving hearts, we prayed corporate forgiveness and absolution over the penitents bowed on the floor in shame and guilt. Then the missionary gave a fiery speech, flooding the room with words and sobs.

Twelve new people stood and walked to the front, stopping behind those weeping in prayer on the floor.

"These twelve will leave tomorrow and take their places," the missionary interpreter explained. "They *are willing* to die for Christ. Pray for them that they will have the boldness and courage of martyrs."

Such radical commitment I have never witnessed in all of my life. Never had I felt more strongly a need for seeing the person and not the deed, a need for forgiveness rather than censure. I felt guilt for not heeding that call. I knew I needed deeper commitment to Christ.

In God's presence, we receive the ability to accept people as they are. Such acceptance isn't easy. We tend to judge the sins in others but find it difficult to be honest in confronting our own sins. Often the very sins we condemn in others are the sins we have the most difficulty confronting in our own lives.

God accepts us. Many talk about God in harsh, cruel, and negative ways. He is pictured as a hardened judge out to condemn people to hell the moment they sin. But in God's presence we discover that he accepts us as a loving parent. God desires to restore, revive, and renew any part of us that has been torn and shattered by mistakes and failures.

God accepts me even when

_____

_____

_____

You may be asking, "What must I do for God to accept me?" The answer is nothing. The invitation of the God who loves is to "come as you are." That doesn't mean he leaves you the way you are. In fact, God loves you too much to leave you as you are. Your untapped potential in life needs to be realized. Your limitless purpose in life must be acted upon. And your past bad habits that limited your present and nullified your future have to be broken. The good news is that the potential God created in you can and will be realized in your life if you will acknowledge the reality of your acceptance.

Acceptance is hard to believe. It's so difficult for some of us to fully believe

God accepts us just the way we are. Why? Because others have told us through the years just how bad we are. Parents and associates tend to focus on what's wrong with us and rarely point out our strengths and possibilities. But God sees us for who we can become, not who we've been. We have nothing to prove to God. He knows all about our past and still he accepts us. The only thing we must change to receive God's acceptance is our rejection of his acceptance.

Accepted without putting others down. In God's presence, we see others from his perspective. We don't have to put others down to feel good about ourselves. No longer do we have to step on others to climb the ladder to full acceptance. Instead we discover that God gives us the ability to accept ourselves without having to judge or condemn others. "Accept one another, then, just as Christ has accepted you in order to bring praise to God."[2]

Letting go of prejudice. Outside of God's presence, we reject others and others reject us. Rejection erodes one's self-image and destroys one's self-respect. Out of rejection grows deep-rooted resentment and prejudice. Hating ourselves, we project our hate on others. To receive God's acceptance in his presence, we must let go of prejudice.

Outside of God's presence, we become legalists. Using law, we quickly judge who is right and wrong, acceptable and unacceptable, good and evil. "Law is a reflection and source of prejudice. It both enforces and suggests forms of bias."[3] Outside of God's presence, we develop prejudices against people based on religion, gender, lifestyle, ethnicity, wealth, and a multitude of other factors. We focus on ways people are different than us and then label the differences as bad.

However, God is no respecter of persons.[4] He treats everyone equally. He accepts everyone as they are. One story by Jesus sums up his acceptance in ways that run counter to our sensibilities.

A master needs servants to work for him. Early in the morning, he hires laborers. He promises them a wage for the day, and they agree. At noon, more workers are needed. The master hires more workers and promises to pay them the same wage as those who started working early in the day. Finally, late in the day, the master hires even more laborers whom he promises to pay the same wage as those who started early in the day.

Of course, when the time comes for all the laborers to collect their wages, the workers who began early see that everyone is paid the same, including those who only worked a few hours at the end of the day. They are incensed, but the master reminds them that they had freely agreed to work for that wage. But they compared themselves to the other workers and felt they had worked harder.

That's the problem with prejudice. Prejudice judges one group of people as better than another group. Outside of God's presence, the only standard for evaluation is another person who is better or worse than we are—by our own estimation. But in God's presence, God himself becomes the only standard to which we compare ourselves. All are lacking and all need his acceptance to dwell in his presence.

With whom do I wrongly compare myself?

_____

_____

_____

KEYS TO INVITING GOD'S PRESENCE

⚷ List things you have difficulty accepting (specific races, lifestyles, sexual preferences, socioeconomic groups). Ask God to help you see them from his perspective.

_____

_____

_____

⚷ Meditate on God's character. Think of all that he has done to accept you. Ask God to conform you to his character so you may become more like him.

⚷ Go to someone whom you find it difficult to accept. Ask forgiveness for your prejudice.

In God's presence, prejudice flees.

Accepted and Aiming to Please

W HOM DO YOU AIM TO PLEASE? IMAGINE YOUR life as a theater stage. Look out from the stage into the audience. For whom are you performing? Whose applause do you relish? Whose approval are you dying to get?

To be accepted, teenagers wear certain clothes, go to popular activities, and act certain ways. Adults are no different. We have our name brands, particular cars, status neighborhoods, civic clubs, political parties, and even particular churches, synagogues, or mosques. We join to belong and to be accepted.

Pleasing God and prospering others. Some have it backwards. They live to please people and try to prosper God. God doesn't need our money. We give offerings, not to please God and gain his favor, but rather to express our love and gratitude. We prosper others because we are blessed to be a blessing.

I please God when I

_____

_____

_____

Pleasing God doesn't begin with trying to do good things to gain his favor. Rather, pleasing God begins with a hunger and desire to be with him. We love being with our children just because we enjoy their presence. The same holds true for being with God. We love his presence and hunger to be with him.

God bestows favor on those who simply enjoy being in his presence. He is pleased with our desire to dwell in his presence. King David sings:

"Blessed are those who dwell in Your house; they will be singing praises to You . . . For a day in Your courts is better than a thousand. I would rather be a doorkeeper in the house of my God than dwell in the tents of wickedness. For the Lord is a sun and shield; the Lord will give grace and glory; no good thing will he withhold from those who walk uprightly."[5]

The religious try to please God by doing. They perform acts of goodness to receive the praise of men not God. Why? "For they loved the praise of men more than the praise of God."[6]

Consider these inquiries:

➤ Have you ever heard someone pray in a way that you knew was aimed to please those listening instead of God?

➤ Have you ever listened to a message, homily, sermon, or speech given to receive the applause of men instead of heaven?

➤ Have you ever read something written to please the reader instead of to motivate the reader to please God?

➤ Have you ever been in the presence of a religious person and felt they were more impressed with themselves than with God?

We give openly to impress people; we give in secret to please God. We make speeches to gain the applause of people; we humble ourselves in prayer to please God. We perform aiming to please people; we worship aiming to please God. That which pleases God rarely attracts the notice of men. We even feign humility to receive praise. Cullen Hightower observed, "Sometimes we deny being worthy of praise, hoping to generate an argument we would be pleased to lose." In the secret closets of the heart we find the rewards of God's presence.

Be especially careful when you are trying to be good that you don't make a performance out of it. It might be good theater, but the God who made you won't be applauding. When you do something for someone else, don't call attention to yourself. You've seen people like that in action—play actors I call them—treating prayer meeting and street corner alike as a stage, acting compassionate as long as someone is watching, playing to the crowds. They get applause, true, but that's all they get.

When you help someone out, don't think about how it looks. Just do it—quietly and unobtrusively. "That is the way your God, who conceived you in love, working behind the scenes, helps you out."[7]

So what pleases God? Desiring to be with God, listening to his voice, hearing and obeying his commands, serving and loving others without a desire to gain reward or recognition—these things please God. So our aim is to please him always in everything we do.[8]

Thinking of all that I have done in the last twenty-four hours, I see my underlying motive has been to please

_____

_____

_____

KEYS TO INVITING GOD'S PRESENCE

🗝 Here is a self-evaluation tool. Use it to evaluate whom you are aiming to please. Check the appropriate column.

MY ACTIONS	MYSELF	OTHER PEOPLE	GOD
When I serve others, I aim to please	_____	_____	_____
When I worship, I aim to please	_____	_____	_____
When I pray, I aim to please	_____	_____	_____
When I join a group, I aim to please	_____	_____	_____
When I give, I am to please	_____	_____	_____

🗝 Enter God's presence and allow him to convict you and bring you to repentance for those times you have performed for others instead of living to please him.

Aiming to please God, we enter in his presence.

Accepted with Favor and Blessing

GOD'S PRESENCE BESTOWS FAVOR AND BLESSING upon us. When we dwell in his presence, favor and blessing become a part of our journey, not a destination for life.

When driving down a freeway, we take for granted the smooth road, the signs clearly marking our way, and the clear road ahead of us. Being in God's presence is like traveling down a superhighway that is built, planned, engineered, and maintained for our safety and comfort. Life in God's presence is filled with his favor and blessings that come, not because we have earned them, but because God has already set them in place for us to enjoy.

We have come to regard the provisions and gifts of God as the blessing. We have even sung songs with phrases like, "Count your blessings, name them one by one." The favor and blessings of God are the fruit, the byproducts if you will, of being in his presence. But the blessing is not the houses, cars, money, status, or possessions we get from God. Rather, the blessing and favor of God is simply this: being in his presence.

Favor comes when we dwell in God's presence.

How have I experienced the favor of God's presence in the last week?

_____

_____

_____

As a child, Jesus enjoyed God's presence. As a result, favor came to him: "And Jesus increased in wisdom and stature, and in favor with God and men."9

Accepted by God, we already have favor and blessing. Our problem is how to appropriate such abundant grace without becoming selfish, proud, arrogant, or rude.

God's favor and blessing is free to enrich our lives when we separate ourselves from those negative, critical, and judgmental people who drain our emotions, sap our strength, and tear down our self-esteem. Imagine the blessing and favor of God in your life as roses. As long as the gardener (God) waters, fertilizes, and prunes the rosebush, you have an abundance of roses—blessing and favor. But leave the presence of the gardener and enter the presence of negative, critical people and watch what happens. They don't water or care for your rosebush. Instead, they pick the roses, crush the petals, and make perfume for themselves. Without the care of the true gardener, the rosebush soon dies, and all you have left are thorns. Outside of God's presence, the roses of blessings and favor cease.

God's presence is a river of blessing and favor. Consider all the creatures in the sea. They are continually nurtured and blessed by the seawater. They swim in a tide of provision and abundance. So do we. In God's river of blessing, we live in favor. King David sings of it this way:

> [God] forgives your sins—every one.
> He heals your diseases—every one.
> He redeems you from hell—saves your life!
> He crowns you with love and mercy—a paradise crown.
> He wraps you in goodness—beauty eternal.
> He renews your youth—you're always young in his presence.[10]

The phrase in the previous Scripture that gives me the most joy is

_____

I feel that joy because

_____

Thankfulness. That's the attitude we have in God's presence. We enter his presence with thanksgiving. We overflow with praise and adoration. The air we breathe, the bread we eat, the clothes we wear, the family we love, the job we work, the car we drive, the place we live—all of these are not the blessing but the fruit of the blessing and favor of God's presence. The blessing is being in God's presence, having an intimate relationship with him. The fruit of that blessing is enjoying all that springs from intimacy with God.

Today I am thankful for

_____

_____

_____

KEYS TO INVITING GOD'S PRESENCE

⚬⟶ What things and associations rob you of God's favor and blessing? List them and then work to separate yourself from their negative impact on your life.

_____

_____

_____

⚬⟶ List the fruit of God's favor and blessing in your life resulting from being in his presence. Then write a prayer of thanksgiving.

_____

_____

_____

In the river of God's presence
flows blessing and favor.

Receiving Mercy and Forgiveness

S O WHY DO YOU CARRY IT? WHY DO YOU CARRY THAT tremendous load of baggage from the past on your back? How is it that you struggle with it? Why do you continue to let it weigh you down?

In seeking God's presence, we find out that we have been carrying a tremendous load, some heavy baggage from the past. In *Ragman and Other Cries of Faith,* Walter Wangerin Jr. spins a powerful tale of a ragman who goes through the streets crying out for people's old, dirty rags. Through his sacrificial life, the ragman transforms the old rags into new, clean garments for us to wear.

I saw a strange sight. I stumbled upon a story most strange, like nothing in my life, my street sense, my sly tongue had ever prepared me for. Hush, child. Hush now, and I will tell it to you.

Even before the dawn one Friday morning, I noticed a young man, handsome and strong, walking the alleys of our city. He was pulling an old cart filled with clothes both bright and new, and he was calling in a clear tenor voice: "Rags!" Ah, the air was foul, and the first light filthy to be crossed by such sweet music.

"Rags! New rags for old! I take your tired rags! Rags!"

"Now this is a wonder," I thought to myself, for the man stood six-feet-four, and his arms were like tree limbs, hard and muscular, and his eyes flashed intelligence. Could he find no better job than this, to be a ragman in the inner city?

I followed him. My curiosity drove me. And I wasn't disappointed. Soon the ragman saw a woman sitting on her back porch. She was sobbing into a handkerchief, sighing, and shedding a thousand tears. Her knees and elbows made a sad X. Her shoulders shook. Her heart was breaking.

The Ragman stopped his cart. Quietly, he walked to the woman, stepping round tin cans, dead toys, and Pampers. "Give me your rag," he said gently, "and I'll give you another."

He slipped the handkerchief from her eyes. She looked up, and he laid across her palm a linen cloth so clean and new that it shined. She blinked from the gift to the giver.

Then, as he began to pull his cart again, the Ragman did a strange thing: he put her stained handkerchief to his own face; and then he began to weep, to sob as grievously as she had done, his shoulders shaking. Yet she was left without a tear.

"This is a wonder," I breathed to myself, and I followed the sobbing Ragman like a child who cannot turn away from mystery. "Rags! Rags! New rags for old!"

In a little while, when the sky showed gray behind the rooftops and I could see the shredded curtains hanging out black windows, the Ragman came upon a girl whose head was wrapped in a bandage, whose eyes were empty. Blood soaked her bandage. A single line of blood ran down her cheek.

Now the tall Ragman looked upon this child with pity, and he drew a lovely yellow bonnet from his cart. "Give me your rag," he said, tracing his own line on her cheek, "and I'll give you mine."

The child could only gaze at him while he loosened the bandage, removed it, and tied it to his own head. The bonnet he set on hers. And I gasped at what I saw: for with the bandage went the wound! Against his brow it ran a darker, more substantial blood—his own!

"Rags! Rags! I take old rags!" cried the sobbing, bleeding, strong, intelligent Ragman.

The sun hurt both the sky, now, and my eyes; the Ragman seemed more and more to hurry.

"Are you going to work?" he asked a man who leaned against a telephone pole. The man shook his head. The Ragman pressed him: "Do you have a job?"

"Are you crazy?" sneered the other. He pulled away from the pole, revealing the right sleeve of his jacket—flat, the cuff stuffed into the pocket. He had no arm.

"So," said the Ragman. "Give me your jacket, and I'll give you mine." So much quiet authority in his voice!

The one-armed man took off his jacket. So did the Ragman—and I trembled at what I saw: for the Ragman's arm stayed in its sleeve, and when the other put it on, he had two good arms, thick as tree limbs; but the Ragman had only one. "Go to work," he said.

After that he found a drunk, lying unconscious beneath an army blanket, an old man, hunched, wizened, and sick. He took that blanket and wrapped it round himself, but for the drunk he left new clothes.

And now I had to run to keep up with the Ragman. Though he was weeping controllably, and bleeding freely at the forehead, pulling his cart with one arm, stumbling for drunkenness, falling again and again, exhausted, old, and sick, yet he went with terrible speed. On spider's legs he skittered through the alleys of the *city, this mile and the next, until he came to its limits, and then he rushed beyond.*

I wept to see the change in this man. I hurt to see his sorrow. And yet I needed to see where he was going in such haste, perhaps to know what drove him so.

The little old Ragman—he came to a landfill. He came to the garbage pits. And I wanted to help him in what he did but I hung back, hiding. He climbed a hill. With tormented labor he cleared a little space on that hill. Then he sighed. He lay down. He pillowed his head on a handkerchief and a jacket. He covered his bones with an army blanket. And he died.

Oh how I cried to witness that death! I slumped in a junked car and wailed and mourned as one who has no hope—because I had come to love the Ragman. Every other face had faded in the wonder of this man, and I cherished him; but he died. I sobbed myself to sleep.

I did not know—how could I know?—that I slept through Friday night and Saturday and its night too. But then, on Sunday morning, I was wakened by a violence.

Light—pure, hard, demanding light—slammed against my sour face, and I blinked, and I looked, and I saw the first wonder of all. There was the Ragman, folding the blanket most carefully, a scar on his forehead, but alive! And, besides that, healthy! There was no sign of sorrow or age, and all the rags that he had gathered shined for cleanliness.

Well, then I lowered my head and, trembling for all that I had seen, I myself walked up to the Ragman. I told him my name with shame, for I was a sorry figure next to him. Then I took off all my clothes in that place, and I said to him with dear yearning in my voice: "Dress me."

He dressed me. My Lord, he put new rags on me, and I am a wonder beside him. The Ragman, the Ragman, the Christ![11]

In God's presence, we receive riches for rags, forgiveness for guilt, purity for impurity and health for disease. "For you know the grace of our Lord Jesus Christ, that though He was rich, yet for your sakes He became poor, that you through His poverty might become rich."[12]

A remarkable exchange happens in God's presence. Instead of giving him our best, which is never good enough, we give him our worst, for that is what he asks for. The baggage, the load of the past, is lifted. In God's presence, we hear his continual invitation, "Come to me, all you who are weary and burdened, and I will give you rest. Take my yoke upon you and learn from me, for I am gentle and humble in heart, and you will find rest for your souls. For my yoke is easy and my burden is light."[13]

The burden of guilt for which I need to receive God's forgiveness is

_____

_____

_____

KEYS TO INVITING GOD'S PRESENCE

⚬⚲ What baggage do you need to throw away in his presence?

_____

_____

_____

⚬⚲ Picture yourself dressed in new, expensive, fine garments in his presence. Imagine the old rags of your past sin, failure, and guilt being thrown away. Describe how you feel.

_____

_____

_____

⚬⚲ Who needs to hear the good news of God's forgiving love from you? When will you tell them?

_____

_____

_____

—⚬⚬⚬—

In God's presence, we are forgiven.

Showing Mercy and Forgiveness

FORGIVEN OF MUCH, WE ARE ABLE TO FORGIVE. When we sow mercy, we will reap mercy from others. That which blocks our ability to forgive is ungratefulness.

The ungrateful live in the shadows of continual offense. They are offended with themselves for not accomplishing more and earning more in their lives. They are offended with others for underpaying and undervaluing them. They are offended with God for not giving them all they believe they deserve.

Offended people find themselves powerless to forgive.

Sometimes, feeling offended has quenched my willingness to forgive an offender by

_____

_____

_____

Offended people often carry offenses for years and hold on to every hurtful action that has come their way. Offended people are cut off from the presence of God. They cannot grasp the meaning of "Your heavenly Father will forgive you if you forgive those who sin against you; but if you refuse to forgive them, he will not forgive you."[14]

Each of us has choices to make between life and death, blessing and curse, forgiveness and offense. Offenses cut us off from blessing, life, and mercy. The only way we can stay offended is to depart from God's presence. Being unforgiving is unforgivable.

Bitter feelings of offense not released often transform genuinely spiritual persons into hardened, religious fanatics. Unable to receive and give mercy, they become harsh judges of others. They constantly condemn the sinners around them while refusing to see their own sin. They condemn others for not praying when they don't pray. They judge immorality in others while living in impurity themselves.

In *The Bait of Satan,* John Brevere accurately observed that offense is the devil's tempting bait. The moment someone hurts us, a trap of offense is laid. We can take the bait and leave God's presence, or we can refuse the bait and show mercy and forgiveness. Religious people are often offended with others. When given the opportunity to be offended, they take the bait.

But those hungering and thirsting after the presence of God refuse the bait. It's not because they are stronger or more righteous than the religious. Humbled in God's presence, they realize how much God has forgiven them. They have heard God say: "I have swept away your offenses like a cloud, your sins like the morning mist. Return to me, for I have redeemed you."[15] Having been forgiven much, those dwelling in God's presence realize that no offense against them can be greater than their past, forgiven offenses against God.

Those dwelling in God's presence have a quality that reflects the One with whom they abide: They forgive. In his presence, it become easier to say "Will you forgive me?" Or "I forgive you." Outside of his presence, the negative options often chosen for responding to hurt are offense, vengeance, and retribution. In God's presence, blessing prompts forgiveness and favor becomes mercy in our lives. Outside of his presence, we live with the curse of offense.

The choice is yours: to curse with offense or to bless with mercy.

Right now I must forgive

_____

_____

_____

🗝 Go immediately to those with whom you are offended. Forgive them and ask them to forgive you for being offended.

🗝 Ask God to warn you whenever the temptation of offense presents itself. Ask for the power to refuse the bait.

🗝 List all that God has forgiven you. Thank him for his forgiveness.

_____

_____

_____

Empowered by God's presence, we refuse offense,
instead showing mercy and forgiveness.

Accepted and Forgiven in God's Presence

I know God accepts me because

_____

_____

_____

Those I need God to help me accept are

_____

_____

_____

I experience blessing and favor in God's presence when

_____

_____

_____

I am grateful to God for his forgiving love in

_____

_____

_____

To overcome the temptation to be offended I need

_____

_____

_____

—∞∞∞—

The wellspring of forgiveness bubbles
from God's presence.

Wholly and Holy in God's Presence

The pursuit of God will embrace the labor of bringing our total personality into conformity with His. . . . Made as we were in the image of God, we scarcely find it strange to take again our God as our All. God was our original habitat and our hearts cannot but feel at home when they enter again that ancient and beautiful abode.

—A. W. Tozer,
The Pursuit of God

Introduction

To walk in God's presence—dwelling, abiding, and living in it—is a life wholly and holy unto him. Each aspect of life becomes immersed in his presence. Life is not like a pie sliced into many pieces with one of the pieces being God's presence. Life is like a pie sliced into many pieces with the crust of every piece being God's presence. His presence saturates every moment, every relationship, every task and every inner longing of our hearts.

God comes to us saying, "Be holy as I am holy." In a practical way, that means dedicating, consecrating, and setting apart everything in life as belonging to and shaped by his presence. Religion makes the various elements of existence sacred while deeming others profane. But God's presence declares that everything in life must be holy—completely surrendered to, ordered by, and in relationship to him.

Living a holy life means that God's presence comes wholly into everything we are and do. *Holy* has the same root as *wholly;* it means complete. A man is not complete in spiritual stature if all his mind, heart, soul, and strength are not given to God.[1]

Inviting God's presence in family. With spouses, children, parents, and other family members, we have the opportunity to be transformed by God's presence from individuals into community.

Inviting God's presence in worship. As we corporately gather with others in worship, we discover that the chief end of man is to glorify and praise God.

Inviting God's presence in work. The liturgy of life moves through the workplace where we cannot ignore the ethics of holiness as we manage our time and make our money.

Inviting God's presence in friendship. The joy of having friends results in the sharing of integrity and companionship and discovering the sacred nature of the friendship that is anchored in God's own presence.

Inviting God's presence in prayer. There is a sacred dialogue of spirit to spirit that only prayer can create. Within us exists a communion closer than any friendship and more intimate than any earthly love—communing with the lover of our souls.

Let us spend this final week considering these five dimensions of life that will be eternally changed by God's presence.

Inviting God's Presence in Family

T HE FIRST HUMAN-TO-HUMAN RELATIONSHIP GOD created was the marital relationship. The first marriage brought about an earthly union that was intended to mirror the divine romance between us and God.

Out of marriage came family. Children and then grandchildren, seeds and then the seeds' seed continued the generations that would either experience the blessings of God's presence or the curse of separation.

Families gathered together into clans and tribes, then communities and peoples, into ethnic groups and nations. We have explored some of the Israelites' journey into God's presence as a family from her early days in the loins of Abraham to her glory days in the Promised Land.

For Christians, the presence of God can be found in the family of God—the church. Corporate gatherings support the fact that everyone is a brother and sister, a spiritual parent and a spiritual child. When one rejoices, all should rejoice; when one suffers, all should experience suffering.

Family brokenness. Separation within families can greatly hinder the presence of God in our lives. Abandonment, abuse, separation, divorce, annulment, and attacks on the family like disease, poverty, war, and death can cause us to build walls between ourselves and God's presence. How? By blaming God for the demise of the family. By turning anger we have for family members toward God.

But God's presence can heal any family brokenness, making the family both wholly and holy in his love and reconciliation. The first ones to see the change that God's presence has made in our lives often are other family members. They know what we have been like. They can discern whether we are changing.

Learning in God's presence to serve one another. The presence of God transforms the way we relate to our family members. The love, mercy, grace, blessing, forgiveness, and servanthood inspired by God's abiding presence can make us instruments of reconciliation and healing within our families.

For years I was religious. As a religious leader, I sought to please my professors, please my congregation, please my board, please my denomination, and please every visitor that walked through the door. In the end, my religion became my mistress and my family a ragtag group of orphans.

Like the prodigal son, one day I came to myself. If God's presence couldn't abide in a family, I certainly would never experience his presence at church, worship, work, or anywhere else. What difference did it make if I gained religious insight and lost family relationships? I returned to my family, sought God's presence, and discovered holiness and wholly living at home.

I am holy and wholly serving at home when

_____

_____

_____

Over the years, various individuals have confided to me, "I must leave my mate and serve God." I have urged them to seek God's presence by serving their mate. "No greater love has any man than this, that he will lay down his life for a friend"[2]—including mates, children, parents, and other family members. Religious people are ready to serve the poor, outcast, homeless, and downtrodden, but often are unwilling to serve their families.

Holiness becomes real when a spouse remains faithful to a mate; when a child honors a parent; when a parent teaches and respects a child; when a family learns to serve one another in the presence of God.

In marriage, family, and parenting conferences, we often ask the participants to turn to their family members and say, "How may I serve you?" Laughter usually breaks out all over the room. After years of expecting family members to serve me, I discovered the joy in God's presence of serving them—my wife, children, in-laws, siblings, and grandchildren. In the context of my service, they have begun to see the presence of God in and through me.

My family experiences God's presence in and through me as

_____

_____

_____

KEYS TO INVITING GOD'S PRESENCE

➤ List different ways you can share God's presence in your family today.

_____

_____

_____

➤ Call or contact an estranged family member and reconcile. How will you do it? When will you do it?

_____

_____

_____

➤ Write a prayer thanking God for your family. Share your prayer with all your family members.

_____

_____

_____

*Serving family members ushers
in God's presence.*

DAY 2

Inviting God's Presence in Worship

GOING TO A WORSHIP SERVICE BECOMES A RITUAL and duty for the religious. They go empty-handed, hoping and praying to be filled. One congregant told me, "I come to worship empty and expect God to fill my cup." How sad. God was waiting and willing to fill her cup every moment of every day. She simply missed it.

Worship is taking God's presence that abides in us and freely sharing it with others through prayer, praise, singing, giving, witnessing, ministering, and serving one another. When two or more gather in his name, God is in their midst.[3] The miracle isn't that God mysteriously shows up when we gather. The miracle is that God is already present before we gather. Our gathering simply allows everyone the opportunity to rejoice, testify, praise God, and celebrate the Presence that continually abides in us.

When I gather with others hungry for God's presence, what do I encounter or experience?

_____

_____

_____

We come to worship not to find his presence but to share his presence. In that sharing, our experience of God's presence is deepened and celebrated. The first step in the act of worship is to relax and to become aware of that upon which we are dependent, that which sustains us in every breath we breathe.

Reread the words to "Breathe," the lyrics that you read when you began this book. This chorus describes the atmosphere in which true worship transpires.

This is the air I breathe,
This is the air I breathe,
This is the air I breathe,
This is the air I breathe,
Your holy presence,
Living in me.

This is the bread I eat,
This is the bread I eat,
The word of life,
Broken for me.

And I,
I'm desperate for you,

And I,
I hunger for you.

And I,
I'm lost without you.

We miss God's presence in worship when worship becomes a spiritless ritual devoid of life and filled with duty.

O come, let us worship and bow down
Let us kneel before the Lord our maker.[4]

Worship in God's presence is filled with:

Tears and laughter,
    Dancing and kneeling,
Testimony and praise,
    Singing and silence,
Words and the Word,
    Giving and receiving,
Miracles and signs,
    Wonders and healing,
Power and grace,
    Conviction and change.

When the people who gather overflow with God's presence, worship overflows with God's presence. Popular religious literature has been filled with guidance on how to be program-driven, policy-driven, people-driven, and purpose-driven. What we need most desperately in worship is to be presence-driven.

I come into worship

_____

_____

_____

KEYS TO INVITING GOD'S PRESENCE

- Prepare to go to corporate worship filled with God's presence. Experience the difference being filled makes.

- Find a partner or partners with whom you can pray and worship. Set times to get together for worship.

- Fill your day with worship music, times of prayer and praise, and opportunities to share God's presence with others through acts of service and kindness, witnessing, giving, and serving.

⎯⎯⎯⎯⎯∞⎯⎯⎯⎯⎯

Worship allows the overflow of
God's presence in our lives.

Inviting God's Presence in Work

MANY MAKE RELIGION A SEGMENT OF THEIR existence and isolate their faith from their work. Once God's presence invades our beings and indwells us, we cannot leave God at church, home, or any other place. God does not dwell in a building. He dwells in us. Consequently, the workplace becomes holy and sanctified, the same as every other aspect of our lives.

God's presence at work. Imagine work being a tabernacle where the holiness of God is real in your relationships and in your contracts, negotiations, or dealings with your colleagues.

I experience God's presence at work when

_____

_____

_____

Work is vocation. Vocation is God's calling on our lives to serve him in the world. That means that every action at work should reflect what God would say or do. Such wholeness at work with God's presence sanctifies every transaction, task, and to-do list with God's presence. Instead of the one-minute manager, we experience God managing our Palm Pilots and Day-Timers with his grace, truth, timing, and priorities. Our moments are so managed by God that all we do carries his mark of excellence, morality, and integrity.

Who is the competition? Work done in worldly ways often focuses on winning and losing. But what if our work attitude is this: my success is helping others succeed. We can make our work meaningful by allowing the character of God indwelling us to motivate everything we do at work.

Work doesn't have to be governed by worry, competition, comparison, and winning. Work can be governed by God's desire for us to serve others and meet their needs. We can earn our wages with hard work and set aside laziness. Laziness steals time—and therefore money—from our companies and employers. God isn't a taker; he's a giver. So we can infect our workplaces with his presence by becoming givers, finding ways to help others win, and serving the needs of others.

God's presence needs to invade our workplaces. That happens initially, not by us vocalizing our religious convictions with religious language, but when God's presence fills our work, when we regard others as loved creatures created by a holy God. We impart holiness through kindness, love, grace, and treating others with dignity and respect. We give our employers the gift of hard work and service because a job done with excellence reflects a holy mindset:

> *"Celebrate God all day, every day. I mean, revel in him! Make it as clear as you can to all you meet that you're on their side, working with them and not against them. Help them see that the Master is about to arrive. He could show up any minute! . . .*
>
> *"Summing it all up, friends, I'd say you'll do best by filling your minds and meditating on things true, noble, reputable, authentic, compelling, gracious— the best not the worst; the beautiful, not the ugly; things to praise, not things to curse."*[5]

A colleague of mine, working in a large corporation, discovered that the man in the office next to him was dedicated to seeking and pursuing God—just as he was. What shocked both men was that they had worked together for over five years without ever mentioning God to one another. Both had so compartmentalized their pursuit of God from their work that both had missed out on an irreplaceable experience—God's presence in the workplace.

God's presence works miracles even at work. Though terribly deformed, Charlie Steinmetz was a mental genius. Few in his day knew more about electricity. Recognizing his ability, Henry Ford hired him. He built the generators for Ford's first assembly plants. One day the generators stopped and production ground to a halt. Henry Ford immediately called on Charlie to find the problem.

Steinmetz fiddled with some gauges, tinkered with some motors, tested some wires and then threw the master switch. Immediately, the plant's assembly lines started up again.

A few days later, Steinmetz mailed Ford a bill for $10,000, a huge sum for that day. Though very wealthy, Ford didn't want to pay such an exorbitant amount for what seemed to be such little work.

Ford wrote a note to Charlie: "Charlie: It seems awfully steep, this $10,000, for a man who just a little while tinkered around with a few motors." Steinmetz wrote a new bill and sent it back to Henry Ford with this note: "Henry: For tinkering around with motors, $10; for knowing where to tinker, $9,990."[6]

Often in my work, I have faced a problem much too difficult for me or my colleagues to solve. After trying everything, I would finally give up and pray. *Then* God would graciously show me the answer. I may know how to tinker to start a job, but only God's presence in my work knows where to tinker to get the job done right. Without God, work lacks meaning, purpose, and direction. With God, nothing at work is impossible!

God's presence in me is shared at my work through

_____

_____

_____

KEYS TO INVITING GOD'S PRESENCE

Trust God's presence to solve a problem at work that you find impossible. After God solves it, write down what he did.

_____

_____

_____

Name a person at work who brings God's presence into the workplace. Give God thanks for that person. What can you learn from that person?

_____

_____

_____

> ⚷ Give your job to God. Celebrate that God is your source of self worth, not your job.

———— ⚛ ————

In the workplace,
share God's presence.

Inviting God's Presence in Friendship

The following scriptural truths echo continually in God's presence:

➤ The righteous should choose his friends carefully.

➤ A friend loves for all times, and a brother is born for adversity.

➤ A man who has friends must himself be friendly, but there is a friend who sticks closer than a brother.

➤ Faithful are the wounds of a friend.

➤ Greater love has no one than this, than to lay down one's life for his friends.

➤ You are My friends if you do whatever I command you.

➤ No longer do I call you servants, for a servant does not know what his master is doing; but I have called you friends, for all things that I heard from My Father I have made known to you.[7]

Which of the above statements touches MY life most powerfully right now?

_____

_____

_____

Inviting and then finding God's presence culminates in friendship with God. He is the best and truest of friends. And our friendship with him is the standard by which all friends and friendships are measured. "The very possibility of friendship with God transfigures life. The religious convictions, thus, tend inevitably to deepen every human friendship, to make it vastly more significant."[8]

Becoming God's friend means that you:

➢ Listen to his voice

➢ Obey his command

➢ Love what he loves

➢ Hate what he hates

➢ Go where he goes

➢ Abide where he dwells

➢ Speak what he speaks

➢ Act how he acts

Such friendship comes with a price. He has paid a high cost on the cross and you pay a high price when you die to self.

What you find in his presence is friendship. With God as your friend, no adversary or adversity in life can defeat you.

To me, friendship with God is

_____

_____

_____

KEYS TO INVITING GOD'S PRESENCE

🔑 Write down qualities of a best friend. Circle the qualities you bring to your friendship with God.

_____

_____

_____

🔑 Think of all the friends God has given you. Contact them soon and tell them how much their friendship means to you.

⊶ Name a friend who does not know God. How can you befriend this person so that he or she can meet your best friend?

_____

_____

_____

—∞—

In God's presence, friendship becomes costly.

DAY 5

Inviting God's Presence in Prayer

In God's presence, prayer is transformed from monologue into dialogue. No longer do we just pray and run. No longer can we just dump our feelings, requests, and needs on God and then leave. Praying in his presence requires times of silence and listening on our parts.

The best time of the day for me to enter into prayer with God is

_____

_____

_____

As in all intimate relationships, abiding in God's presence means that a great deal of communication happens without words. There is a knowing that comes in his presence that tells us God's will before we express our wants.

What is prayer? William James in *The Varieties of Religious Experience* gives this description: "The very movement itself of the soul, putting itself into a perfect relation of contact with the mysterious power—of which it feels the presence."[9]

In God's presence, prayer becomes more an expression of his concerns than ours.

In God's presence, prayer focuses more on others than ourselves.

In God's presence, prayer ceases to be complaining and becomes crescendos of praise.

In God's presence, prayer connects the invisible with the visible, the impossible with the possible, and the eternal with life-changing moments.

In God's presence, prayer flows boldly in expressing all of our feelings, including our doubts along with our faith.

In God's presence, prayer makes holy the mundane and makes humble the proud.

In God's presence, prayer focuses on what God can do instead of on what we cannot do.

In God's presence, his Spirit prays through us when we fail to have the words to pray.

In God's presence, prayer resurrects the corpse of existence and breathes into us the breath of Life.

In God's presence, life becomes prayer. "Pray constantly, give thanks in all circumstances."[10]

In God's presence, I pray

_____

_____

_____

KEYS TO INVITING GOD'S PRESENCE

🗝 Listen to God. Be still. Now pray.

🗝 Listen to God. Write down what you hear. Now pray.

_____

_____

_____

🗝 Pray for others. Ask God how to pray for others. Ask God how your life can be an answer to the prayers of others. Write down what God says to you.

_____

_____

_____

Life and prayer unify into one breath in God's presence.

Wholly and Holy in God's Presence

In a paragraph, describe how you are now inviting God's presence into your life daily.

_____

_____

_____

Write down 5 key words that describe how you experience God's presence.

_____

_____

_____

List the names of those with whom you need to share God's presence.

_____

_____

_____

⸺⸺✦⸺⸺

God's presence invites dialogical prayer.

What's Really Needed

Awaking in the middle of the night
With sweat pouring from my pores and worry flooding my consciousness,
I cried out to God with my questions.
What I thought I needed was answers.
What I really needed was God's presence.

Holding the hand of a dying stranger,
I groped for what to say before he crossed the divide from time into eternity.
What I thought I needed were the right words to say.
What I really needed was God's presence.

Praying for the woman in front of me dying with terminal cancer,
I struggled with a prayer that would give her comfort
And me a release to move on to an easier problem to pray for.
What I thought I needed was a quick prayer.
What I really needed was God's presence.

Counseling with the angry couple before me,
I searched for viable, positive options that might save their marriage.
What I thought I needed was the perfect counseling tool to help their marriage
*   heal.*
What I really needed was God's presence.

Worshipping in the midst of thousands, prepared to speak with power,
I poured over my notes in a last minute refresher
Hoping to not forget the main points.
What I thought I needed was a message.
What I really needed was God's presence.

*Debating the proof of God's existence with a stranger seated next to me on the
  plane,
I racked my memory for the teleological, cosmological, and ontological
  arguments for God's existence.
What I thought I needed was the clinching point that wins debates.
What I really needed was God's presence.*

*Struggling at my keyboard to write a manuscript of profound meaning and
  impact,
What I thought you needed was another book.
But in the final analysis,
What you really need is God's presence.*

This journal is completed, but your journey is just beginning. For your continuing
pursuit of God's presence, I pray:

*May God's presence bless and protect you. May his presence smile on you daily
and fill your moments with grace. May his presence favor you with every good and
perfect gift. May his presence guide you in the paths of peace now and ever more.
Amen.*

Introduction
1. Mark 10:15 (TLB)
2. Acts 17:24
3. See Psalm 139:7–8

Week One
1. Psalm 46:10
2. Matthew 7:14 (TLB)
3. Psalm 86:5
4. Jeremiah 31:3 (NIV)
5. See Genesis 12:1
6. Isaiah 28:23–24; John 10:27-28; Jeremiah 39:18 (NIV)

Week Two
1. Isaiah 55:8–9 (TLB)
2. See Genesis 1:26
3. See Genesis 3:56
4. Genesis 3.8
5. Psalm 22:1–2 (NIV)
6. 2 Corinthians 4:18 (NIV)
7. Buber, Martin. *I and Thou* (New York: Simon & Schuster, 1970). p. 11.
8. Mark 10:18 (NIV)
9. Genesis 3:8 (NIV)
10. Abraham Maslow, *Motivation and Personality* (New York: Harper & Row, 1956).
11. Genesis 3:6 (TLB)
12. 1 Corinthians 13:12 (TLB)
13. Judges 18:6
14. Genesis 1:26
15. Jeremiah 29:11–12 (TLB)
16. 2 Corinthians 9:10 (TLB)
17. Jeremiah 31:3
18. Deuteronomy 31:6
19. Cyril Connolly. *Unquiet Grave* (1944), pt. 2.
20. Psalm 16:11 (NIV)

Week Three
1. 1 John 3:19–20 (NIV)
2. Matthew 5:21–22 (TLB)
3. Alexander Yelchaninov, *Fragments of a Diary*
4. Ephesians 4:26–28
5. See Genesis 4:14

6. Genesis 4:16
7. Psalm 139:1–10
8. Psalm 46:10
9. Luke 17:21 (TLB)
10. Matthew 7:26–27 (TLB)
11. Numbers 23:19
12. Genesis 11:4
13. Deuteronomy 10:17
14. Psalm 51:10–11
15. Brother Lawrence, *The Practice of the Presence of God* (Grand Rapids, MI.: Fleming H. Revell, 1958), 70.
16. James 4:8–10 (NKJV)
17. See Genesis 11:7
18. Romans 3:23 (TLB)

Week Four
1. David W. Moore, "Most American Workers Satisfied with Their Job: One-Third Would Be Happier in Another Job," Gallup Poll News Service (August 31, 2001), http://www.gallup.com/poll/releases/pr0108 31.asp, available to subscribers only.
2. Genesis 2:24 (NIV)
3. Malachi 2:15 (TLB)
4. Numbers 6:24–26
5. 1 Corinthians 13:4–7 (TLB)
6. Deuteronomy 6:5–9 (NIV)
7. Deuteronomy 4:37
8. Acts 17:24–25
9. See Isaiah 43:18
10. See Isaiah 43:18, 2 Corinthians 5:17
11. See Mark 2:22
12. Romans 8:28 (NIV)
13. See http://www.teamtechnology .co.uk/tt/t-articl/midlife.htm
14. Harvey Deutschendorf, *Men and Work* (National Consultation on Career Development [NATCON], 1997).
15. Numbers 13:32–33 (TLB)
16. See Matthew 16:4
17. Exodus 33:14–16
18. John 1:4 (NIV)

Week Five
1. See 2 Kings 19
2. See Numbers 13:27–28

3. Isaiah 48:6
4. Numbers 11:1 (TLB)
5. Numbers 12:10
6. See Exodus 17:8–16
7. Psalm 22:1–2, 14–15
8. Numbers 21:17–18
9. John 7:37–38
10. John 6:32–33
11. Deuteronomy 2:33–34
12. Deuteronomy 30:19–20
13. Psalm 27:1,5,8
14. Exodus 20:4–5
15. Exodus 13:21–22
16. Exodus 33:15
17. Jeremiah 29:11–13
18. Galatians 5:22–23
19. Leviticus 11:45
20. Job 11:7–9 (NIV)
21. Deuteronomy 13:4–5
22. Jeremiah 1:3
23. Leviticus 20:26

Week Six
1. See Judges 17:5–6, 8:34–35
2. See Psalm 119:2
3. 1 Kings 8:10–11
4. Matthew 22:37–39, adapted
5. Colossians 4:5–6
6. Matthew 11:28–29 (TLB)
7. See Psalm 133 (NIV)
8. Psalm 16:11
9. Psalm 21:6–7
10. John 17:21 (KJV)
11. Isaiah 61:1–2
12. Psalm 139:1, 6, 23–24

Week Seven
1. Psalm 51:1–2, 9–11
2. Luke 12:16–21
3. Matthew 19:16–22
4. Matthew 6:7 (TLB)
5. See John 10:10
6. Song of Songs 2:10–13
7. Proverbs 11:28
8. Ecclesiastes 4:10
9. See Matthew 18:20
10. See Acts 1:4, 2:1

11. See Matthew 25:40
12. See John 15:15
13. Matthew 7:1–6 (NKJV)
14. Matthew 19:17
15. W. H. Auden, *New Year Letter*
16. Mark 4:22–24 (TLB)
17. Romans 3:23
18. Isaiah 1:18–20
19. John 14:6
20. See 1 John 4:4
21. 1 John 3:20–21 (NASB)
22. Matthew 7:1
23. John 8:7
24. John 16:8 (TLB)

Week Eight

1. Viktor E. Frankl, *Man's Search for Meaning* (New York: Washington Square Press, 1959), 137–138.
2. Deuteronomy 6:4–5
3. Romans 7:18–21
4. Ephesians 2:4–9 (TLB)
5. Psalm 139:13–16 (RSV)
6. Acts 17:26–28
7. See Acts 2:38
8. John 1:10–13
9. See Mark 7:13
10. Hebrews 10:18–20 (TLB)
11. John 15:13 (NIV)
12. Romans 5:8–11 (TLB)
13. John 14:9
14. 1 Corinthians 3:16–17 (TLB)
15. Romans 13:8–10 (TLB)
16. 2 Chronicles 6:41–7:3
17. 2 Corinthians 4:6–7

Week Nine

1. Matthew 18:19–20 (TLB)
2. John 15:4–5
3. Sam Hinn, *Changed in His Presence* (Creation House, 1995).
4. See 1 Kings 18–19
5. See Acts 17:4
6. See 1 Corinthians 3:16–17; 6:19
7. See 1 Kings 19:13
8. Jeremiah 17:23
9. Tilden H. Edwards, *Spiritual Friend*
10. Matthew 21:28–31 (TLB)
11. John 12:50 (TLB)
12. James 4:8
13. See Isaiah 43:18–19
14. See 2 Corinthians 5:17

15. Isaiah 43:19 (RSV)
16. John 16:13 (NIV)
17. John 15:9–10
18. John 15:4
19. See Galatians 5:22–23
20. 1 Corinthians 13:4–8 (NIV)
21. F.W. Faber, *The Spirit of Father Faber*
22. Romans 5:1 (TLB)
23. Romans 5:3–4 (TLB)
24. Romans 8:31
25. See Philippians 2

Week Ten

1. Prairie Public Broadcasting and Dr. Ron Pies, M.D., Ask the Expert, 10/29/2001, http://www.mhsource.com/expert/index.html and http://www.prairiepublic.org/features/healthworks/depression/stats.htm
2. Arnold Joseph Toynbee, *An Historian's Approach to Religion*
3. Thomas à Kempis, *The Imitation of Christ*
4. John 15:13 (NKJV)
5. "Victory in Jesus" paraphrased
6. Eric Fromm, *The Sane Society*
7. M. Scott Peck, *The Road Less Traveled*
8. Ezekiel 11:19–20
9. 2 Corinthians 5:17–18 (The Message)
10. 2 Corinthians 7:9–10 (The Message)
11. Matthew 5:4
12. Matthew 5:4 (The Message)
13. 2 Corinthians 1 (The Message)
14. 2 Corinthians 1:3 (TLB)
15. 1 Peter 5:7 (NIV)
16. 1 Samuel 17:47 (NIV)
17. See Psalm 7:10
18. Exodus 17:12–13, 15–16 (NIV)
19. Romans 8:38–39 (TLB)
20. John 1:1–5 (The Message)
21. 1 Corinthians 15:56–58 (The Message)
22. P. A. Sheehan, *Mary, the Mother of God*
23. James 1:17–18
24. Malachi 3:6
25. Viktor Frankl, *Man's Search for Meaning*
26. See Romans 8:28
27. Psalm 23:4 (KJV)
28. Isaiah 53:4–5 (NIV)
29. 1 Peter 1:6–7 (The Message)

30. Psalm 37:24 (NIV)
31. See Malachi 3:2
32. David A. Redding, *Jesus Makes Me Laugh with Him*
33. 1 John 4:19 (NIV)
34. Revelation 3:20 (The Message)
35. A. W. Tozer, *The Pursuit of God* (Camp Hill, PA: Christian Publications, 1982), 61.
36. 1 John 4:7–12 (The Message)
37. Helen Mallicoat, quoted in Tim Hansel, *Holy Sweat*
38. Matthew 25:44–45

Week Eleven

1. Matthew 7:1
2. Romans 15:7 (NIV)
3. Diane B. Schulder, *Sisterhood Is Powerful*
4. See Acts 10:34
5. Psalm 84:4, 10
6. John 12:43
7. Matthew 6:1–4 (The Message)
8. 2 Corinthians 5:9 (TLB)
9. Luke 2:52
10. Psalm 103:3–5 (The Message)
11. Walter Wangerin, Jr., *Ragman and Other Cries of Faith* (San Francisco: Harper Collins, 1994). Used by permission.
12. 2 Corinthians 8:9
13. Matthew 11:28–30 (NIV)
14. Matthew 6:14 (TLB)
15. Isaiah 44:22 (NIV)

Week Twelve

1. R. J. H. Steward, *Spiritual Conferences of R.J.H. Steward*
2. See John 15:13
3. Matthew 18:20
4. Psalm 95:6 (RSV)
5. See Philippians 4 (The Message)
6. Charles R. Swindoll, *The Tale of the Tardy Oxcart,* (Nashville: Thomas Nelson, 1998) 322, adapted.
7. Proverbs 12:26, 17:17, 18:24, 27:6, John 15:13–15
8. Henry Churchill King, *The Laws of Friendship*
9. William James, *The Varieties of Religious Experience*
10. 1 Thessalonians 5:17 (RSV)